D1859814

HANGING BY A THREAD:
AFGHAN WOMENS RIGHTS AND SECURITY THREATS

HANGING BY A THREAD:
AFGHAN WOMENS RIGHTS AND SECURITY THREATS

Dr Massouda Jalal & Dr Mario Silva

GYAN

© **Author**
All rights reserved. No part of this work may be reproduced, stored, adapted, or transmitted in any form or by any means, electronic, mechanical, photocopying, micro-filming, recording or otherwise, or translated in any language, without the prior written permission of the copyright owner and the publisher. The book is sold subject to the condition that it shall not, by way of trade or otherwise, be lent, resold, hired out, or otherwise circulated without the prior publisher's written consent in any form of binding or cover other than that in which it is published.

The views and opinions expressed in this book are author(s) own and the facts reported by them have been verified to the extent possible, and the publishers are not in any way liable for the same.

ISBN : 978-81-212-1330-1

Price : ₹ 630

Originally Published in North America by Mosaic Press, 2014

Republished in 2016

Gyan Publishing House
5, Ansari Road
Daryaganj, New Delhi-110002
Phones: 9811692060
E-mail: books@gyanbooks.com

Printed at: G. Print Process, Delhi.

Cataloging in Publication Data—DK
Courtesy: D.K. Agencies (P) Ltd. <docinfo@dkagencies.com>

Jalal, Massouda, 1967- **author.**
Hanging by a thread : Afghan women's rights and security threats / Dr Massouda Jalal & Dr Mario Silva.
pages cm
ISBN 9788121213301

1. Women's rights—Afghanistan. 2. Women—Violence against—Afghanistan. 3. National security—Afghanistan. 4. Peace-building—Afghanistan. 5. Postwar reconstruction—Afghanistan. 6. Humanitarian assistance—Afghanistan.
7. Afghanistan--Politics and government—2001- I. Silva, Mario, 1966- author. II. Title.

HQ1236.5.A3J35 2016 DDC 323.3409581 23

Contents

PART–II

Afghan's Rights and Security Transition Post 2014

Preface

The book, HANGING BY A THREAD: AFGHAN WOMEN'S RIGHTS AND SECURITY THREATS, is a result of meeting Dr Massouda Jalal during my visit to Afghanistan between June 25–30, 2010, with a delegation of human rights campaigners from Canada led by the president and founder of One Free World International, Reverend Majed El Shafie.

During our visit we had an opportunity to meet several members of the Afghan government, including the Minister of Foreign Affairs, the Minister of Education, and one of President Karzai's senior advisors.

Dr Jalal was kind enough to invite us to her foundation, and we spent several days meeting with individuals of domestic violence and child abuse, and other victims of human rights violations. Her foundation is very active in the protection and promotion of women's human rights and undertakes advocacy and lobbying on their behalf.

Although Dr Jalal was a member of the Karzai government, she has always stressed her independence and is a leading critic of the Afghanistan government's failure to advance the social, economic, and political rights of women. During my terms as Member of the Canadian Parliament, I had several opportunities to invite her to speak to parliamentarians and before the Foreign Affairs Sub-Committee on International Human Rights. Dr Jalal is a board member of the International Forum for Rights and Security, which I chair.

The book is divided into two parts. Part I introduces the history of women's struggle in Afghanistan before and after the fall of the Taliban—the human rights challenges and the need to build an enduring peace with women's full participation.

Part II focuses on the issues of security, state failure, the application of international law, terrorism, and the structures and supports that need to be in place following the United States' military withdrawal by December 2014.

—Dr Mario Silva

Part–I

The Long Struggle for Women's Rights in Afghanistan

Dr Massouda Jalal

Introduction

I remember you...

when you gain your rights, reach your goals and hope(s)
but the path is hard, full of obstacles, you must learn how to cope
to cope while struggling for your ultimate goal
a reborn woman, free, independent and whole.[1]

Once again, the women of Afghanistan are hanging by a thread, and our nation is at a crossroads. Now, just when the country is beginning to slowly move forward, Afghans are expected to independently accomplish something that over ten years of massive international support could not achieve—to put an end to the war. I would like to share with you a part of this frightening reality; namely, the perspectives of those who are not being heard back home, laying bare the urgent security issues that Afghan women face as we transition towards sustainable peace.

Our government's vision of sustainable peace is framed in a strategy with twin agenda: (1) to bring back the so-called moderate Taliban into the mainstream of national life and (2) to grant political concessions to their leaders. Women have been excluded from the process of conceptualizing this strategy; however, through informal channels we have raised our concerns regarding its wisdom and viability.

First, Afghan women know that democracy and Talibanism cannot coexist because they are antithetical to one another. Democracy is based on the rule of law, human rights, coexistence, and the protection of human life. Conversely, Talibanism is based on despotism, repression, tyranny, and the glorification of violence. Democracy can only thrive where peace is present, whereas Talibanism can only thrive where violence reigns. Thus, to assume that the Taliban will embrace peace is an unforgivable mistake. And further, to hope that they will make peace under democratic terms is to ignore their ideological makeup. Expecting Afghanistan to make peace with the Taliban that operate both in our country and in Pakistan is like expecting the world to make peace with Al Qaeda.

Have you ever asked yourself what it feels like to have Al Qaedans living in your very midst—in your neighborhoods, local businesses, government agencies, or places of worship? Do you think that making peace with the Taliban will bring about sustainable peace? If, by now, Afghans do not realize that the concept of peace held by the Taliban and Al Qaeda vetoes the democratic concept of peace, then we have lost the very essence of our statehood.

Today, our women face the nightmare of a resurgent Taliban regime. We are bewildered by the sudden obsession of our elected leaders and NATO officials to negotiate peace with the Taliban using a strategy of (1) paying off the 'moderates' to return to mainstream life and (2) giving political concessions to the 'hard cores.'

Second, every Afghan woman knows that there is no such thing as a moderate Taliban. The life experiences of those who have become members of the Taliban have been as uniquely edifying and compelling as the experiences that have made us lovers of peace and democracy. Nothing could genuinely convince a Taliban that terrorism is immoral and that democracy is good for the majority. To make peace with the Taliban is to allow them to erode the very foundations of democracy, which in the past decade have allowed us to live in relative freedom and harmony.

Third, long before our government even thought of reintegrating them into society, the Taliban had already realised that mainstream society was the best tactical ground from which to launch terrorist operations. If complex attacks with horrific results continue to occur, it is because the Taliban are now seamlessly assimilated into families, police departments, the armed forces, businesses, the government, and perhaps even international agencies. Our government certainly does not need to spend large amounts of money to bring them back into society. Tactically, they are already within our midst and are quickly multiplying with skillful invisibility.

Fourth, the seed of Talibanism flourishes in an atmosphere of poverty, hopelessness, oppression, and, most especially, weak leadership. Afghans lack the kind of leadership that could inspire and draw support from all sectors. Our people will not support a president with a long list of credibility issues—ranging from election fraud, clandestine alliance with lawbreakers, graft and corruption, dishonesty and incompetence. Afghans cringe at the thought that substantial amounts of money provided by the international community to the peace process should be channeled to a government that ranks third on the list of the world's most corrupt governments.[2]

Fifth and most importantly, Afghans believe that a peace process should be pursued from a position of strength. Today, it appears that our government has been granting concessions to the Taliban without receiving anything in return. If the Taliban are committed to the process, they should be asked to immediately halt all armed hostilities. Afghans need peace to make peace. Every concession that the government gives to the Taliban should be reciprocated with an equivalent act of peace. Our government's first request of the Taliban should be to immediately stop offensives, bombings, and all acts of violence while negotiations are taking place. The Taliban should agree to adopt a zone of peace, a peace moment,[3] or some rules of engagement that protect civilians from violent acts.

Much ground has been covered in the past decade to bring some relief to the women of Afghanistan. But many activists, social workers, and government and nongovernmental organisations (such as the Jalal Foundation, which I founded) are deeply disappointed and vexed with the way women have been shouted out of the political process—not just by the current Afghan government but also by its international supporters. Many of the gains achieved in the early days after the fall of the Taliban have been slowly clawed at and scraped away. The battle for equality is still not over by a long shot. Women are still being forced into marriage and getting raped and beaten. There are clear signs of a government backslide over issues concerning the status and protection of women's rights and well-being.

The government of Afghanistan as well as the international community need to ensure that the progress that has been made and the rights that women have attained thus far continue to grow and mature, and that the initiatives that are in the pipeline are in harmony with Afghan values and not rooted in the Taliban tradition.

I was recently asked to speak at the Young Atlanticist Summit on the topics of peace, democracy, and gender, and although I was not able to attend, I did provide them with my report. In my report, I noted that Afghanistan has been in the forefront of global news since the fateful 9/11. The world knows that our victorious fight against the Russian invasion culminated in a reign of terror under the Taliban government. We defended our country against Communism but unwittingly fell into the hands of the most tyrannical government ever known to the current world. In wartime, Afghans lived with unbridled hope that peace would follow. But under the Taliban, Afghans lived in terror, and women were transformed into virtual inanimate objects. The reign of the Taliban strangled our freedoms, chained our souls, starved our intellect, and imprisoned our dreams.

The support of the international community helped us win back democracy. For a decade, our nation basked in intermittent peace, and women breathed a faint scent of freedom. The past decade helped us grow as a nation of people who recognize that there can be no substitute to peace if we want democracy and that only under the reign of democracy can we attain gender equality. We learned that peace, democracy, and gender equality are inextricably interlinked and that they are the very foundations of a human-centered society. We need peace to sustain democracy; we need democracy to attain gender equality; and we need gender equality to nourish peace and democracy.

Democracy, human rights, and gender equality are the cornerstones of enduring peace and progress in Afghanistan. However, in a context of complex socioeconomic and political challenges and where peoples' lives continue to hang in the balance in a harsh fundamentalist culture, laying these cornerstones has been an onerous, all-time struggle.

Afghans of today have inherited thought and behavior patterns that sharply distinguish status, roles, social claims, entitlements, rights, opportunities, and many other things in life on the basis of gender and cultural and religious stereotypes. These beliefs and behaviors have perpetuated divisions among people, resulting in the subordination and oppression of the weak; the strong not only dominate the weak but also perpetrate atrocities against them. The situation has been disastrous for the powerless, including women, the poor, ethnic minorities, and those who are victimized by the perverse interpretation of Islam and religious teachings.

Afghan women, in particular, have suffered. The combined impacts of cultural, religious, and gender prejudices have reduced their status to worthless human beings without rights who can be exploited and oppressed, particularly by the very people who are supposed to be their source of strength and protection—their family members. Nowadays, with the anticipated departure of international supporters by the end of 2014, Afghan women are fighting a fierce battle to protect the gains that they won during the last decade. Foremost in our agenda is the preservation of the 2009 Law on the Elimination of Violence against Women, which serves as women's main source of protection against twenty-two acts of violence that are currently punishable under law. The recent resurgence of Taliban influence in the country's governance institutions threatens to help abrogate this law and leave Afghan women defenseless against the extreme cruelties that are committed against them. In the absence of this law, women could only hope for a better future if the next generation of Afghans is taught to unlearn religious, cultural, and gender prejudices that are instrumental to women's oppression.

Indeed, our inability to advance economically and politically is rooted in Afghanistan's sick social structure. We need to overhaul it in such a way that renders inequalities, religious extremism, and lawlessness anachronisms. Afghanistan should breed a fresh generation of people who would unequivocally stand for freedom, peace, good governance, and social justice. We need to breed an army of young women and men who will put a stop to the intergenerational transmission of ideologies that make religion, gender, and culture a justification for terrorism, violence, banditry, social inequity, the suppression of rights, and all forms of injustices that make the lives of Afghans regressive and miserable. We need nontraditional leaders who can bring unity to our people, heal the wounds of our battered past, and bring everybody into a collective journey forward.

A holistic, systematic approach is not always possible, especially in a messy context like Afghanistan. However, a good starting point would be to bring together related initiatives, identify achievements and strengths, point out obstacles and ways to address them, and draw up a holistic strategy based on the given situation. It is an imperative that such strategy includes advocacy at the highest levels and the engagement of progressively thinking religious leaders. They are a rare breed and are likely to face serious antagonism from their colleagues. For this reason, broader support will have to be solicited (for example, from the Organisation of Islamic Countries).

Transforming a society is always a difficult, arduous journey that takes several generations to achieve. But it can be done, and we should begin now. With the resurgence of fundamentalism in Afghanistan, the educational system should stand as an incorruptible frontier for nonprejudiced behavior, thought patterns, and culture. The situation of our country cannot change by waging only a physical war against the enemies of our people. More, the real war should be fought in the minds of our people, especially hanging by a thread: part i the next generation. It is this single, attainable factor that keeps the hope of our women alive.

In the meantime, in this book that I am coauthoring with Dr Mario Silva, I take the opportunity to appeal to the international community to continue to support the Afghan women's struggle to protect their rights and well-being. Help us keep the Elimination of Violence against Women Law safe from manipulation and possible abrogation by fundamentalist supporters in our parliament. Let the light of hope visit our land again and bring wisdom to our leaders and decision makers. Let optimism live on, especially in these most trying times in the life of Afghans.

Notes

1. Poem by Dr Zieba Shorish-Shamley entitled *I Remember You.* Available at: http://www.afghan-web.com/woman/ziebapoem5.html
2. According to Transparency International's 2011 Corruption Perception Index, Afghanistan ranks third among governments that are perceived to be most corrupt.
3. A peace moment may be a day, a week, or a month without initiating an act of confrontation from both parties.

Chapter 1

The History of Women's Struggle in Afghanistan

The rickety socio-political forces upon which Afghanistan is built are a weak and perverse reflection of its rugged, uneven topography. The history of Afghanistan's women reinforces the belief that of all countries, Afghanistan is the worst for women to be born in. Afghanistan's roots are firmly embedded in gender bias, and the country has been fertile ground for women's struggles over the ages.

The widespread mayhem that has resulted from the social, political, and economic disruptions mushrooming in every corner of Afghanistan has affected particularly the women in society; they are doomed to lead dreadful lives. Women's issues are an integral part of the nation's heritage, so much so that they have shaped an entirely unique identity for Afghanistan. Nonetheless, the women of Afghanistan are not set apart from the country's remaining institutions. To a large extent, the fate of women is decided by ethnic values mingled with varied interpretations of Islam.

What could depict the plight of Afghanistan's women better than the 2003 Afghan Women's Bill of Rights? Despite the assurance of a number of political leaders, it was not included in the constitution. Or the *jirga's* (an assembly of tribal leaders) conference that began with the chairman, Sighbatullah Mojadeddi, addressing the assembly of women:

> We all have to respect the vote. Women are free to vote for men. Men are free to vote for women. We cannot make this separation...

Do not try to put yourself on a level with men. Even God has not given you equal rights because under his decision two women are counted as equal to one man.[1]

In 2006, the *loya jirga*[2] (grand council) took a step towards giving women their much deserved equal rights. The move proved another fake promise in the *naqaab* of hope. The equal rights clause stated that "men and women have equal rights and duties before the law." However, it would have flown against the nature of Afghanistan's male-oriented society if the law was true to its word. The clause remained equivocal since it was kept open to interpretation for the purpose of undermining women's rights.

Historical Perspectives

The current situation of Afghan women paints such a dismal picture that one cannot imagine that they ever enjoyed any rights or freedom on the soil of Afghanistan. Surprisingly enough, history has a different tale to tell. Women have been the heart and soul of Afghanistan. They have driven it forward, shaping the course of its history and forming an integral part of its destiny. Sadly, their contributions are poorly documented in Afghan history books.

Nineteen-year-old Malalai, Afghanistan's Joan of Arc, is an Afghan national heroine who does feature in school books. She is famous for her role in the battle of Maiwand during the second Anglo-Afghan war. Her father, a shepherd, and her fiancé both joined the war alongside Ayub Khan in 1880. Like many other Afghan women at that time, Malalai tended the wounded.

When the tide turned against the Afghan warriors and morale seemed to be dropping, she is said to have cried out:

Young love, if you do not fall in the battle of Maiwand
By God someone is saving you as a token of shame.[3]

When the Afghan flag bearer was shot dead, Malalai used her veil as a banner to encourage the Afghan fighters. She sang:

With a drop of my sweetheart's blood,
Shed in defense of the Motherland,

Will I put a beauty spot on my forehead?
Such as would put to shame the rose in the garden.[4]

Malalai was shot and killed in the battle of Maiwand. Legend has it that it was her wedding day. She died, but her words gave courage to the Afghan soldiers, who went on to win the battle. After the battle was over, Malalai was honored for her courage and buried in her native village, Khig. Today, there are many hospitals, schools, and other institutions that have been built in Malalai's honor and bear her name.

How did a woman like Malalai, a warrior on the battlefield, become one of Afghanistan's greatest heroines, given that today's Afghan women have a hard time even stepping outside the front door without their husbands' permission or a male escort?

Abdur Rahman Khan 1880–1891

Times weren't always gloomy for the women in Afghanistan, 1880 to 1901 brought about a change in women's status in society. During his reign, Abdur Rahman Khan, "The Iron Amir," attempted to consolidate the nation into a centralised state for the very first time. Paradoxically, this ruthless ruler acted as a change agent and introduced some amendments to certain customary laws concerning women, particularly those dealing with marriage. He gave women the right to divorce under certain circumstances, a decision that was both offbeat and advanced for the times. He raised the marriage age of girls and abolished the tribal tradition of forcing a woman to marry her deceased husband's brother. Women were also given the right to inherit property during his reign.

On the death of Abdur Rahman Khan, his son Amir Habibullah Khan took over the throne and reigned for eighteen years. Amir Habibullah Khan brought back the Afghan exiles. One of them was Mahmud Beg Tarzi, an Afghan nationalist and intellectual, whom Amir Khan's father had sent into exile. It was under Tarzi's influence that Amir Habibullah Khan opened a school for girls, which even boasted an English curriculum. Indeed, Mahmud Tarzi introduced a number of significant changes. The light of modernisation shone especially brightly in Afghanistan between 1911 and 1918. During that time, Tarzi advocated education and supported political diversity. Unlike others, he was convinced that women had great potential; they were a boon to society, and Islam did not deprive them of equal rights. Tarzi thus believed that women deserved equal treatment in society and that full citizenship was their due. His outstanding contribution to Muslim women was a special section in his newspaper *Seraj-ul-Akhbar—Celebrating Women of the World.*

Amanullah: Era of Social Transformation 1919–1929

In the year 1919, Amanullah succeeded and began his rule in Afghanistan. He was inexorable in modernizing Afghanistan. Being largely influenced by Tarzi and leading by his example of educating and giving equal opportunities to the women in his family, Amanullah embarked upon the work of uplifting women in society.

His wife, Soraya Tarzi, Queen of Afghanistan, was Mahmud Tarzi's daughter. She worked diligently for women's freedom and rights and became the most influential woman of her time. She helped and supported Amanullah in his modernisation efforts in the face of stiff resistance from the tribal and religious elements of society. A number of women from Amanullah's family participated in government meetings and also joined as government officials.

During this period polygamy was discouraged. Amanullah was against keeping women behind closed doors and veils. At a public function he is known to have said:

> Religion does not require women to veil their hands, feet and faces or enjoin any special type of veil. Tribal custom must not impose itself on the free will of the individual.[5]

In 1920, Amanullah's sister Kobra set up an organisation for women's protection, called Anjuman-e-Himayat-e-Niswan. The organisation pushed for women's unity, encouraged Afghan women to voice their complaints and fought injustices and oppression of women. Amanullah's other sister set up a hospital for women. Queen Soraya started the first women's magazine in Afghanistan, *Ershad-e-Niswan* (Guidance for Women). It wasn't long before the old-fashioned tribal leaders revolted and fought against the freedoms that were advocated by the king and queen.

The year 1926 saw Afghanistan celebrating its seventh anniversary of independence. Soraya took the opportunity and addressed the masses:

> It [independence] belongs to all of us and that is why we celebrate it. Do you think, however, that our nation from the outset needs only men to serve it? Women should also take their part as women did in the early years of our nation and Islam. From their examples we must learn that we must all contribute toward the development of our nation and that this cannot be done without being equipped with knowledge. So we should all attempt to acquire as much knowledge as possible, in order that we may render our services to society in the manner of the women of early Islam.[6]

However, events took a backward turn after Amanullah and Soraya returned from a trip to Europe in 1928. Conservative mullahs disapproved of photos of the queen, who appeared in them without a veil as she dined with foreign men. The royal family was met with hostility on their return, and their downfall proved imminent.

Conservative Afghans complained that Amanullah's reforms were extremely "Western" and contrary to the doctrines of Islam.

Late 1920s and 30s

It was not until the late 1920s that the traditionalist and rural leaders came out in full protest at the Westernised reforms. The 1920s was marked by a growing rift between the modernist and traditionalist tribes. The traditionalists became especially incensed in 1921, when women were given the right to marry a partner of their own choice, and in 1924, when the bride price was forbidden.

The *loya jirga* was infuriated when the marriage age of girls was raised to eighteen years and for men, to twenty-one years. The abolition of polygamy was another shock. By the late 1920s, women were not allowed to attend school and had to revert to covering themselves with a veil. Amanullah had to succumb to the changing beliefs of society, which were eating away at the well-established values of liberty and equality.

After the fall of Amanullah, consecutive leaders did very little to bring about real change for women. The laws and reforms that were introduced were contradictory in nature. The period was one of discrimination and illtreatment of women.

The rule of Nadir Shah (1930s) brought some respite; however, Nadir Shah was assassinated in the year 1933. Nadir Shah gave in to the demands of the tribal and religious leaders and cancelled many of the reforms put in place by Amanullah and Soraya. He banned *Jarideh Zanan*, which was the only newspaper being published by women. His main concern was to keep the tribal leaders at bay.

Mohammed Zahir Shah 1933–1973

Zahir Shah was the last king of Afghanistan, reigning for four decades, from 1933 until he was ousted by a coup in 1973. His reign saw a slow and gradual change for Afghan women. In 1941, for example, the first secondary school was set up for girls in Kabul.

Mohammad Daoud Khan, Zahir Shah's cousin and his prime minister from 1953 to 1963, was a reformist. The technical assistance coming from the Soviet Union in the 1950s further helped Afghanistan on its journey of modernisation. The focus sharpened on women's education, and Afghan women started entering the workforce. They became nurses, doctors, teachers, and even politicians..

During 1959, women were allowed to appear in public without veil; the wives of the ruling family and senior government officials attended public functions without veils. A revolt in Kandahar over this issue was successfully quelled.

In 1964, Afghan women got the right to vote and were allowed to enter politics. The Democratic Organisation of Afghan Women (DOAW) was formed the very next year and started working against forced marriages, bride pricing, and illiteracy. In 1968, Queen Soraya died in exile in Rome, Italy.

Pre Soviet Period 1973–1978

Mohammad Daoud Khan's presidency (1973–1978) was marked by a continuation of his progressive and liberal policies, and urban women enjoyed many rights and personal freedom. In 1977, the female activist Meena Keshwar Kamal was able to lay the foundations of the Revolutionary Association of the Women of Afghanistan. They were bold enough to criticize the Mujahedin for war crimes after the Mujahedin had freed Afghanistan from the Soviet Union. The Revolutionary Association of the Women of Afghanistan has since been supporting secular governments as opposed to Islamic ones.

In contrast to urban areas, rural areas remained narrow minded and backward, and women living there continued to be exploited, oppressed, and treated like property.

Daoud's rule in Afghanistan is best captured in his own words:

> We will never allow you to dictate to us how to run our country and whom to employ in Afghanistan. How and where we employ the foreign experts will remain the exclusive prerogative of the Afghan state. Afghanistan shall remain poor, if necessary, but free in its acts and decisions.[7]

With Communism flexing its muscles, Daoud was unable to successfully carry out economic or social reforms. In 1965, the People's Democratic Party of Afghanistan (PDPA) had been formed. By 1978, the PDPA's power was in full swing; with the backing of the Soviet Union, it was running the show, and it introduced large scale social reforms in Afghanistan. The PDPA encouraged mass literacy for men and women, age no bar, and a decree was issued for the compulsory education of girls. The marriage age of girls was increased to 16 years and that of men, to 18 years. The bride price was abolished completely.

Communist ideology accompanied the liberal ideology and lifestyle that were propagated by the PDPA. Brute force was used to implement the PDPA agenda, and there was little, if any, tolerance at all for tribal and religious sentiments. The mishandling and disregard of tribal and religious customs caused resentment and, in turn, a backlash. The PDPA moved swiftly and brutally, killing scores of people.

Following Daoud's assassination by the PDPA, Nur Mohammad Taraki, its leader, established the Democratic Republic of Afghanistan and declared himself president. Once he had seized power, Taraki continued the work of promoting and establishing full women's rights.

Life under the Soviets 1979–1989

When Soviet Russia invaded Afghanistan, many Afghans were killed by the Communist government and its Russian allies. Numerous women and children were also killed, yet at the same time Afghan women had access to basic freedoms. They were accepted and encouraged to work in universities, airlines, as well as private corporations. Some women went further; in 1984, Khatol Mohammadzai became Afghanistan's first woman paratrooper and later achieved the rank of general in the Afghan army. As all other reforms that had women at their core, the ones introduced by the PDPA were deemed unwarranted by conservative traditionalists. Some even considered them to be an "unbearable interference in domestic life." The reforms were met with large-scale killings of PDPA reformers and the shooting and killing of women wearing Western clothes in Afghanistan.

Needless to say, women's rights were at this time tightly wedged within a communist framework. An Afghan girl, Nahid, helped organize a large demonstration against the Russian occupation. She brought together girls from different schools in and around Kabul. Nahid was killed and became a symbol of martyrdom and patriotism. She is famous throughout Afghanistan. Meena Keshwar Kamal (founder of the Revolutionary Association of the Women of Afghanistan) was assassinated in 1987.

Decline of the Soviet

In 1989, the Soviet Union ended its long and iron rule in Afghanistan. But the Soviet withdrawal was no cause for joy. The country became an easy target for civil wars, and an era of chaos began. Between 1989 and 1992, Afghanistan was rent by the war between the Mujahideen and the communist government of Najibullah. Very little social development or changes took place during this period.

Mujahideen

In 1992, the Mujahideen seized power from the Communists, taking over in Kabul, and set up an Islamic state; it now lay in the hands of those who considered women to be weaker and subordinate to men. The Mujahideen established laws and rules strictly formulated according to Islam, and their entry into Afghanistan was followed by the ruthless and thoughtless burning of universities, libraries, and schools.

Civil war continued. The murder, mayhem, and violence that resulted were not limited to women alone; abuses and gross violations of human rights were inflicted on the general Afghan public. Yet, despite all the massacres and mass killings, Afghan women were allowed to pursue an education and to work. Under the Mujahideen government of Burhanuddin Rabbani, half of Kabul's workforce was made up of women. They worked as doctors, teachers, secretaries, nurses, and in numerous other professions.

As it took over the reins from Rabbani in 1993, the Gulbuddin Hekmatyar administration immediately placed restrictions on women's freedom. But, even then, women were allowed to attend school and to work.

Taliban

The moment the Taliban took over Afghanistan's capital city, Kabul, in 1996, further drastic restrictions were imposed on women. They were forbidden from appearing in public without a *mahram*. A *mahram* is a male whom a woman can never marry because of a close relationship, such as a brother, a father, a sibling. The *mahram* is the guardian an unmarried woman can call upon when necessary, before whom she need not don a hijab; once married, her husband becomes her *mahram*. Whenever a woman stepped out in public, she had to wear a veil. She could not wear makeup and high heels (since no man should hear a woman's footsteps and get excited). She was not allowed to speak loudly in public (as no stranger should hear a woman's voice). All ground and first floor windows were to be painted over or screened so that women should be invisible to any onlookers in the streets. Women were not allowed to appear on the balconies of their houses and apartments. They could not be photographed or filmed; their pictures could not be published in books or newspapers, and were banned from shops and private homes. Women could not visit a male doctor. Worse still, they could not go to school.

The word "women" was to be used carefully; for example, "Women's Garden" was renamed "Spring Garden." Women's presence was banned from television, radio, and all public gatherings. Women were banned from riding bicycles or motorcycles, even with their *mahrams*, nor were they allowed to ride in taxis without their *mahrams*. Special women's buses meant they would not travel with men.

The Taliban rule was the worst period in the history of Afghan women. The women who were doctors and lecturers were reduced to begging and prostitution to feed their families. Such happenings had never before occurred in the entire history of Afghanistan.

In the 1990s, I was working as a psychiatrist and pediatrician, and teaching at Kabul University as a member of the Faculty of Medicine. In 1996, the Taliban government threw me out. I then received an offer to work for the United Nations World Food Programme. During the Taliban regime, I was never involved in politics; instead, I focused my efforts on humanitarian activities.

9/11: The Fall of the Taliban

Towards the end of 2001, the United States and NATO Allied Forces attacked the Taliban and Al Qaeda, and forced them out of Kabul. Women could once again work and attend school. The restrictions placed on them by the Taliban were officially lifted.

On December 5, 2001, my friend Dr Sima Samar was selected as the first Deputy Chair and Minister of Women's Affairs in the Interim Administration of Afghanistan under President Hamid Karzai. She was later appointed Chairperson of the Afghanistan Independent Human Rights Commission.

Malalai Joya garnered international attention when she was elected to the *loya jirga*, which was convened to ratify the Afghan Constitution. She made a powerful speech criticizing her compatriots and calling them war criminals. She raised questions regarding the legitimacy of such warlords being members of the *loya jirga* rather than being put on trial for their crimes. Her accusations were directed at the Mujahideen leaders who had fought against the Russians.

Shortly after the fall of the Taliban, I began speaking out about women's rights and became more active in politics; I became a representative of the Kabul area at the *loya jirga* in 2002. At the time, my name was under consideration for the interim presidentship of Afghanistan. I came in second to Hamid Karzai, with support from 171 of the 1575 delegates. In October 2004, I was appointed Minister of Women's Affairs and served until July 2006. I became vocally critical of the Karzai government for not significantly advancing the social position of women.

Regarding Afghanistan's power structure, I remained an outsider, and I stressed my independence from the warlords and past oppressive regimes. Although many of the candidates for the Afghan presidency withdrew from the race and called for a boycott of the election following reports of voting irregularities at some polling places, I was one of the few candidates who did not join the protest. During the 2005 election, I decided to stand for president, a huge challenge in this male-dominated society. In the end, I received 7 per cent of the vote among Afghans. My candidacy gave Afghans a valuable lesson not to take women for granted and that truly women are men's equal.

In 2004, the country was proclaimed as an Islamic republic and adopted a new constitution according to which the "citizens of Afghanistan—whether man or woman—have equal rights and duties before the law." This constitution also required that half of the members appointed by the president to the *Meshrano Jirga* (upper house of the bicameral National Assembly of Afghanistan, alongside the House of the People, the *Wolesi Jirga*) should be women. In 2006, President Hamid Karzai asked me to join his government as Minister of Women's Affairs. Afghanistan's first ever female provincial governor was appointed by President Karzai in 2005. Habiba Sorabi started her post as governor of the central Bamiyan province in March 2005.

After the Taliban's brutality, I was especially elated and proud to see two female athletes taking part in the Olympics for the first time in Afghanistan's history; Friba Razayee and Robina Muqum Yaar represented Afghanistan in Athens.

In February 2008, Fatima Nazari launched National Need, a party dedicated to women's issues and rights. It was the first political party of its kind. The education of girls was vigorously opposed by the Taliban, and their attacks continued as the female ratio in schools reached 35 per cent. Taliban supporters sprayed acid on the faces of Kandahar schoolgirls, a brutal act that stopped many Afghan parents from sending their daughters to school.

By 2010, the few gains that had been made were slowly being eroded. A controversial Shia personal status law was published in *Gazette 988*, the official Afghan gazette. All personal affairs of Afghanistan's Shia Muslims were covered by this law: marriage, divorce, separation, inheritance, and much more. The law repressed women and was seen as a violation of Article 22 of the Afghan Constitution, which states that the "citizens of Afghanistan— whether man or woman—have equal rights and duties before the law."

> However, [the 2010 Shia law gives] "a husband the right to withdraw basic maintenance from his wife, including food, if she refuses to obey his sexual demands." It grants guardianship of children exclusively to their fathers and grandfathers. It requires women to get permission from their husbands to work. It also effectively allows a rapist to avoid prosecution by paying "blood money" to a girl who was injured when he raped her.[8]

An even more repressive version of the Shia law was ratified by President Hamid Karzai but had to be placed on hold due to worldwide condemnation. This version required Shia women to seek their husband's permission before leaving their own home, unless it was for some urgent work, and required women to have sex with their husbands at least once every four days.

The 2004 constitution guaranteed equal rights for women. In 2009, violence against women became a crime. But in reality, women are still mistreated on a large scale. They continue to live in fear and are the subject of harassment, threats, violence, and at times, murder and torture. Forced marriage and domestic violence are rampant and considered part and parcel of daily life; four hundred women are behind bars for fleeing violent husbands, abusive in-laws, or rape. Although education has been made available to females, less than 40 per cent go to school, and every two hours an Afghan woman dies of pregnancy-related complications.

Violence against, and exploitation of, women has its roots in tribal teachings on the role of women in society. Women have nowhere to run nor any escape routes. Many tribal leaders want to dictate a subservient status for women, and despite continuous and brave attempts at freeing themselves of this tyranny, success has so far eluded them. The continued armed conflict has made women's position worse.

Human rights enjoyed by Afghan women are few and far between. What little rights they do have are often usurped by an exchange system; the women become barter in the hands of their families, clans, and tribes as they settle scores or pursue other vested interests. In a statement issued on July 13, 2012, Under-Secretary-General and Executive Director of UN Women Michelle Bachelet observed that Afghanistan had been witness to cases of extreme abuse and appalling violence against women.

Notes

1. Amy Waldman, "Women are half of men", The New York Times, 16 December 2003.
2. Loya jirga in the Pashto language means "grand council." A loya jirga is a mass meeting usually prepared for major events such as choosing a new king, adopting a constitution, or discussing important national political or emergency matters. In Afghanistan, the loya jirga was originally attended by the Pashtuns, but later included other ethnic groups.
3. http://www.garenewing.co.uk/angloafghanwar/biography/malalai.php
4. *Ibid.*
5. Quote taken from Orzala ashraf Nemat Century Foundation report (2011) on Afghan Women At the Crossroads: Agents of Peace—or Its Victims? Available at: http://www.peacewomen.org/assets/file/Resources/NGO/hr_afghanwomen atthecrossroads_march2011.pdf
6. Louis Dupree, *Afghanistan,* Princeton: Princeton University Press, 1973 at 46.
7. Samad Ghaus, The Fall of Afghanistan, Brassey's (UK) Ltd; 1 edition, 1988 at 178–180.
8. ONEFREEWORLD report on Women Rights in Afghanistan and Pakistan, April 2012 Available at: http://www.onefreeworldinternational.org/wp-content/uploads/2012/06/2012-USC-print-dbl-sided.pdf

Chapter 2

Human Rights

Perhaps it is best to start this chapter with a poem by Dr Zieba Shorish-Shamley, which best encapsulates my sad thoughts on the constant, daily attacks on women and their dignity that I have witnessed. The poem is entitled "I Remember You…"

I remember you…

when you have no choice, no voice, no rights, no existence
when you have no laughs, no joy, no freedom, no resistance
your pain, your agony, your silence, your loneliness
your anger, your frustration, your cries, your unhappiness

I remember you…

when you are abused, attacked, beaten and veiled
when you are tortured, strangled, choked and almost killed
you feel numbness, nothingness, lifelessness and tears
your are a shadow, a ghost, a creature with many fears

I remember you…

when you in the darkness, stillness of a star-less night
lift your arms to the sky, with sadness and fright
and ask the universe with eyes full of tears and pain
why all these crimes? for what reason? can anyone explain?

I remember you…

when you finally will rise and stand on your feet!
and say "No! I will not stand for anymore defeat!"

you will break the chains, burn the veil and destroy the walls!
you will scream with all your might "Damn you all!"

I remember you...

when you take the solemn oath that you will struggle, resist and fight
that you will gain your freedom with all your might
that you will never give up, no matter how heavy the cost
never again will you be confused, pitiful and lost

I remember you...

when you gain your rights, reach your goals and hope(s)
but the path is hard, full of obstacles, you must learn how to cope
to cope while struggling for your ultimate goal
a reborn woman, free, independent and whole.[1]

The act of accusing a woman of adultery, rendering a guilty verdict, and gathering people to execute her is NOT about justice. It is NOT about correcting a mistake, eradicating evils, or making peace. More importantly, it is NOT about religion.

Public execution of women is about oppression of the powerless. It is about injustice. It is about perpetuating a mistake, sustaining evil, and creating reasons for the destruction of peace. More than this, public execution is a murderous act of mass indulgence. People participate because they experience an emotional high, a surge of unparalleled thrills, excitement, anger, guilt, shame, and bewilderment—a mix of emotions that are not experienced in everyday life. The euphoria of immense self-gratification is so overwhelming that people are not aware of what is happening to them. Nevertheless, one thing is certain—subliminally, they crave it more and more. Around-the-clock, every Afghan woman is at peril from the society in which she lives.

All people who love peace, democracy and human rights must stand together against Talibanism. This situation cannot be won with guns, prisons, or policy alone. The battle is a spiritual one against brutish savagery. Afghans need to promote spiritual maturity by training our people, especially the next generation, to embrace a life where conflicts are managed without killing one another.

Many of our people still operate from the distorted paradigm of righteousness that the Taliban left behind. For example, how can Afghans simultaneously believe that adultery is wrong and that killing the victim of adultery is right? A woman who is powerless to resist sexual advances is not adulterous. She is a victim. But in the Taliban's distorted view, she alone is the criminal. Does murdering her brutally in front of a cheering crowd resolve anything? What happens to the men involved in the adultery charge?

My appeal to my fellow Afghans is for us to pause as a nation and ask ourselves how much these Talibanist paradigms still command our spirit. Our society needs spiritual healing to purge itself of the Talibanist ways of thinking and behaving. Afghans may not be with the Taliban in the mountains, but if we allow Talibanist mores to become rooted within us, then we become their followers.

I have made several statements calling upon the government to pursue Talibanism from a combative, military standpoint. The Jalal Foundation, which I founded in 2009 as a nonprofit organisation, was from its inception all about protecting women's rights. I wanted this foundation to help carry out significant work by empowering the female section of society and mobilizing support for uplifting women; and any myths regarding the Taliban as partners in peace had to be dispelled. Eradicating Talibanism begins within each of us. This is a time for national spiritual reflection. Afghans need to provide themselves with tools for self-reflection in order to determine how much of what they believe belongs to Taliban ideology. Afghans need to revisit the content of Afghanistan's school curriculums, the messages of our preachers, and the actuations of our leaders—and obliterate the spiritual space occupied by Talibanism within our midst.

Eliminating Violence Against Women

The Law of Elimination of Violence Against Women (EVAW) was implemented in Afghanistan in August 2009. For the first time in Afghan history, crimes like child marriage, forced marriage, forced self-immolation, and a number of other acts of violence against women were criminalised and made punishable.

In November 2011, the UN Assistance Mission in Afghanistan published a report named "A Long Way to Go: Implementation of the Elimination of Violence against Women Law in Afghanistan." The report showed that there were no comprehensive official statistics pertaining to the cases of violence against women in Afghanistan since most cases were unreported. There were 2,299 cases registered by the Afghanistan Independent Human Rights Commission from 21 March 2010 to 21 March 2011. Based on that number they found that

> prosecutors in 28 of Afghanistan's 34 provinces opened cases in 26 per cent (594 cases) of an estimated 2,299 incidents, filed indictments in seven per cent (155 cases), with primary courts relying on the EVAW law as the basis of their judgments in four per cent (101 cases) of an estimated 2,299 incidents.[2]

Even the cases that do get filed, and in which charges get framed, stand a miniscule chance of a solution or just conclusion; it is very difficult indeed for an uneducated woman living in a remote area of the country to find proof of the crime. Huma Safi, who is the program manager for Women for Afghan Women, based in New York, noted that the "most corrupt system in our country is the system of justice. We have good laws. They are very good...written in the documents, but they are not good in the implementation."

Safi describes a case in which a woman was raped by an Afghan policeman. The court put him in jail for seven years, but the appeals court changed the verdict from rape to adultery, and the man was released but the woman was sentenced to three years in jail. According to Safi, most cases get thrown out of court or dismissed because the women are unable to provide proof of the crime.

The tribal courts and the arbitrary justice systems that mostly handle these cases are heavily biased and based on traditional, male, chauvinistic concepts. The justice done through any of these systems is often the outcome of individual judge's twisted view. Those who dare to sympathize with these victims—judges, lawyers, advocates—are threatened constantly and have to work in fear and under the pressure of the more conservative elements of society.

My organisation has helped young girls who have suffered the brutality of the Taliban. I remember the story of a seventeen-year-old girl who had been kidnapped and raped by a local policeman and two other men. We fought for prosecution, and as a result, the men received long prison sentences. Now, the judges are receiving death threats. I have personally received several death threats.

So I worry about the time when the Western forces have left, and the women have lost what little protection they had. The Afghan government is already beginning to curb the women's rights that were won immediately following the removal of the Taliban from power. No doubt, whatever arrangement the Karzai government makes will jeopardize the hard-won women's rights in Afghanistan.

Women activists are right in their fear. We have accused the present government of Hamid Karzai of losing steam and backtracking on enforcing the already enacted laws that favor women. Women are feeling increasingly vulnerable as the date of withdrawal for the foreign forces draws closer and closer.

It was not long ago that the Afghan Justice Minister termed the women's shelters as dens of prostitution and announced that twelve-year-old girls are of marriageable age. To hear a government minister say such offensive and loathsome things is appalling. Such words are no different to those of the Taliban.

Having faced brutality in all spheres of society, Afghan women have never really expected complete peace and security in their homeland. The lucky ones who have escaped Afghanistan have experienced amazing peace for the very first time in their lives. In 2006, President Karzai approved the Action Plan on Peace, Justice and Reconciliation. However, no law or action plan can ever free Afghanistan from the clutches of injustice and insecurity. Sexualised violence has accompanied each and every war in Afghanistan. There have also been uncountable incidences of war-related rape. Women are threatened from all quarters. The tragedy is that if they speak up, they are beaten to death, and if they stay quiet, their lot in no way improves, nor are they respected for their silence.

According to a 2006 report by the Revolutionary Association of the Women of Afghanistan, the

> security situation in Afghanistan is critical. It is like a ticking bomb, and it is very possible that at any time a civil war will break out. Women and girls have been particularly affected by the insecurity. There are hundreds of attacks on teachers, students and schools across Afghanistan, with girls' schools being particularly hard hit. In most remote villages there are not even any signs of schools for girls. Hundreds of Afghan women have committed suicide due to these intense pressures and hopelessness. When the entire nation is living under the shadow of guns and warlordism, how can its women enjoy their basic freedoms?[3]

The same report also mentions an increase in the number of police for the protection of women in Afghanistan. Women members of parliament are provided with bodyguards, cars, and drivers for securing them against attacks. The report concludes that violence against Afghan women prevails largely because of gender bias. Not only is the violence structural in nature, it is also domestic and has been taking place in both public and private spheres. According to the report (as per the Afghan Independent Human Rights Commission report),

> more than 50 per cent of women have experienced violence within the family. Pervasive violence has led to hundreds of women committing suicide by self-immolation, a problem prevalent across the country but particularly acute in Western Afghanistan. This trend is a testament to the perception by women victims of violence that they have no hope of escape from abuse. Afghan women's organisations have reported that in the past year, several deaths of women as a result of violence have gone uninvestigated by authorities.

Asking for justice and security for women in Afghanistan is like asking for water in the desert. There is simply no possibility, not even the slightest chance, of being treated fairly. A 2003 report by the Revolutionary Association of the Women of Afghanistan, aptly titled "Afghanistan: No Justice and Security for Women," notes that

> [d]espite the lifting of rules limiting their freedom of movement, women are prevented from seeking redress because of barriers in

society and in the community in many areas. Even when a woman is able to approach the police or the courts, she faces extreme discrimination.

The people of Afghanistan (both men and women) have been actively and diligently working towards security of the nation and its women. The focus is on preventing violence and safeguarding women because it is being realised that Afghanistan as a nation will never be able to prosper if its women are not treated with equality and dignity.

Several reports have found that violence against Afghan women is on the rise and that the authorities are unwilling and unable to protect women from violence. In some Taliban-controlled areas, women are constantly harassed and threatened.

Article 54 of the 2004 Afghan Constitution states that the government is required to adopt measures to eliminate negative practices that endanger "the physical and physiological well-being of the family." However, widespread corruption within the judicial system exists and the practice of trading women for marriage to resolve a dispute or debt is still common in some rural areas.

Chairperson of the Afghan Independent Human Rights Commission, Dr Sima Samar, has said, "In the last seven months, four thousand cases of domestic violence were reported in Afghanistan." She believed that male domination and the lack of education are responsible. Samar, however, acknowledged that the "condition of women in Afghanistan has improved a lot since the fall of the Taliban. During the Taliban rule, women were practically imprisoned in their own houses." The Taliban continue to be a threat, as they burn girls' schools and even assault them. "Nonetheless, girls are taking the risk of going to their schools."

Women face incredible challenges when starting their own businesses. For example, twenty-five-year-old tech entrepreneur Mahboob is the CEO of Afghan Citadel Services, an IT firm she founded in the western city of Herat. Her staff of twenty software programmers—more than half of them women—develops computer software for government ministries, universities, and international organisations in Afghanistan.

But in this deeply traditional country, success for women also comes fraught with danger. Mahboob says she has received abusive phone calls and e-mails, warning her to stop working and threatening to target her family.

Mahboob notes:

> Women face many challenges. Even when they have great ideas they cannot start up their own businesses. Women also face insecurity...They can't go and work in the districts or villages. Women have traditional and cultural [challenges]. When you're working, people want to stop you so you can't continue your work.[4]

Afghanistan remains deeply conservative and male dominated. Domestic abuse is routine, forced marriages are the norm, and women are discouraged from pursuing careers. Suicide rates among women are among the highest in the world. So not surprisingly, Mahboob's success as a businesswoman has sparked a fierce backlash from her community. She is constantly changing her phone number and e-mail address due to the threatening calls and messages that she says she receives almost daily. Her father has been supportive. But even he is often confronted by locals who tell him it is dishonorable for his daughter to be working in public, meeting male clients, or even driving a car.

Two of Mahboob's female employees have already resigned under pressure from locals.

Mahboob has also had to overcome considerable market discrimination. She says potential Afghan clients, many of them men, often laugh and express skepticism that she is actually a CEO. Some refuse outright to do business with her company:

> When we go to [potential] customers, they don't believe that women can do [business]. They give you a smile or they look at you as though you cannot [deliver]. Even if they want your product, they want you to give it to them for a price that is cheaper than [the price charged by] a male competitor.

But despite the obstacles, Mahboob and her business have thrived. Afghan Citadel Services currently has ongoing or finished projects worth approximately US$500,000. Among the projects that the company has completed are a patient-management system, created for Afghan hospitals, and a student-registration system for universities and private schools.

Recently, the company has opened new offices, including one in the capital, Kabul. Mahboob has also hired more staff to meet needs as the company's business expands. The company is also expanding into other sectors. Earlier this year, it partnered with Film Annex, an online film distribution platform, to launch the Afghan Development Project. The project seeks to show "a new face" of Afghanistan by broadcasting current, events-related videos, interviews, and news clips. Her company is also working with Film Annex to equip Afghan schools with Internet access in order to connect students with the outside world—and to discourage them from joining the insurgency.

But for Mahboob, it isn't just about business and the bottom line. She says that her main goal is to become a role model for Afghan women. "My message to Afghan women is that they should be ready to change their lives. They [can't] stay at home and say, 'We are just women and we have to stay at home and we accept it,'" Mahboob says. "We have to understand that we have rights. We can bring a lot of changes to society and can bring peace and prosperity to the economy of Afghanistan."

My foundation, the Jalal Foundation, has mobilised Afghans throughout the country; we are gathering one million signatures of support to stop violence against women in Afghanistan and all over the world. We published an Afghan *Women News Digest* to reiterate our plea for the elimination of violence against women and girls and as an expression of solidarity with the global campaign One Billion Rising to Stop Violence Against Women.

When I started the campaign to stop violence against women, I joined the international community and the women of the world in commemorating the International Day for the Elimination of Violence against Women. I called the world's attention to the escalation of violence against Afghan women, which obviously signals a reversion to the Talibanist oppression of Afghan women in the recent past. We condemn and are outraged by the increasing incidents of public executions, beheadings, murders, rapes, beatings, and other forms of violence against Afghan women. More specifically, we hold the Taliban responsible for the seventeen incidents of poisoning that victimized two thousand school girls in various parts of the country in 2012. What a clear act of criminality, one that betrays the degree to which the Taliban feels threatened by the increased status of women.

We need to remind Afghans and the West that violence against women is a violation of human rights, a form of gender-based discrimination, a misuse of power, and more importantly, a criminal act that is punishable under law. I say the West because it pays lip service on this issue and rarely raises it with the Karzi Government. We call upon the Afghan government to perform its duty of protecting the rights of women and girls. The president and his cabinet need to act and use the power given to them by the people to prevent all forms of violence against women and punish all its perpetrators. Having ratified the Convention on all forms of discrimination against women, the government of Afghanistan has an obligation to create the conditions for the full enjoyment of women's rights, including an efficient police and justice system that could serve as a deterrent to violenceagainst-women offenders. Imprison all such offenders and impose on them the punishment that they deserve under the law.

We hail the courage of violence-against-women victims and survivors who stand up to seek justice despite the odds of an unsupportive judiciary and a hostile public opinion. It is your strength that keeps our advocacy alive. You are assured of the continuing support of women's organisations, including the Jalal Foundation and its fifty-member NGO, and Women's Council members nationwide. Your courage will serve as inspiration to our girls to continue the campaign for peace and freedom beyond our lifetime.

To the international community: the war in Afghanistan is not yet over. The Taliban are returning into the mainstream of life, encouraged by the government's peace and reintegration program. We see criminals returning who once killed, tortured, and murdered women without being prosecuted. The return of the Taliban is emboldening communities to ignite the fire of female-directed cruelty and violence. We urge you to continue your vigilant watch on the violation of human rights in this part of the world. Establish an independent international human rights watch group in Afghanistan to document and expose all human rights violations, including violence against women. Withdraw your support for mechanisms of the state that fail to perform competently in protecting women's rights. Most importantly, hold our government accountable for its failures in protecting women's rights.

Today, we stand in solidarity with the One Billion Rising Campaign to Eliminate Violence against Women globally. We are soliciting at least one million signatures of commitment to end violence against women in Afghanistan. One day is not enough—but one day, like today, is enough to move many spirits forward.

Seventeen per cent of women have reported sexual violence, as many as eighty per cent of marriages are forced, and eight million women and girls aged between fifteen and forty are suffering from depression.

A 2009 study, "Gender–based Violence in Afghanistan" by Wazhma Frogh of the Afghan Women's Network, Kabul, made the following observations:

> 87.2 per cent of Afghan women and girls are faced with at least one form of sexual, physical, economical, psychological abuse in Afghanistan. Reported cases of violence against women have increased 100 per cent between 2008 and 2009 ranging from domestic abuse to honour killing to rape to self-immolation and exchange of women to solve communal disputes. Up to 80 per cent of marriages are forced marriages on girls and 57 per cent of girls are forced into marriages without their consent.[5]

Rashida Manjoo, the expert charged by the UN Human Rights Council with investigating and reporting on violence against women, its causes, and consequences noted that the

> killing of women is indeed a State crime when tolerated by public institutions and officials—when they are unable to prevent, protect and guarantee the lives of women, who have consequently experienced multiple forms of discrimination and violence throughout their lifetime.[6]

Afghanistan and the Pakistan Pashtun region are the least likely places where one would want to be a woman. One in fifty Afghan women dies during pregnancy or at child birth. An estimated nine out of ten women are illiterate. On average, a woman has five children. As a medical doctor, the fact that one out of ten children die before their fifth birthday horrifies me. Life expectancy in our country is one of the lowest in the world.

More than 50 per cent of Afghan girls are married or engaged to be married by the age of ten, and by the time they are sixteen, 60 per cent are married. Most of us who work in the field have observed that almost 80 per cent of marriages that take place in rural Afghanistan are either arranged or forced. Girls are often married to men who are much older—sometimes even in their sixties—and the girls usually meet them for the first time on their wedding day. The problem of rape and kidnapping prompts many families to force their daughters to marry at a young age. Marrying a daughter off early means parents avoid the cost of raising her, and the older and wealthier husbands often pay a good sum as the bride price. Girls who get married do not continue their education and usually become mothers as young teenagers, which is one of the main reasons for such a high death rate during pregnancy and child birth.

Afghanistan has one of the highest numbers of widows in the world— an estimated 1.5 million—due to the long-lasting war and conflict, and the deaths of older husbands before their much younger wives. The average age of an Afghan widow is thirty-five. In traditional tribal areas, the elders insist that women stay at home and leave the house fully covered and accompanied by a male relative. Sadly, even in the major cities, many women wear the burqa, not for religious reasons but for fear of family and neighbors. Since most women live in extended families, they are often subjected to abuse and slavery at the hands of their in-laws. As per the Islamic Sharia law, a woman's testimony is worth half of a man's testimony, and children are usually awarded to their fathers or grandfathers in the case of divorce or during custody battles.

The law clearly states that violence against women is a crime and that perpetrators shall be punished. Article 4 of the Elimination of

Violence Against Women Law (EVAW), published in the official gazette on August 1, 2009, states that this law is based on both the Islamic Sharia and the Afghan Constitution. Actions that are forced and cause harm or damage to a woman's body, mind, soul, or property are criminal, be they committed at home, at government or nongovernment institutes, in educational institutes, in public places, on public transport, or in any other place.

According to Article 27 of the Afghan Constitution, the purpose of the law is to

- Safeguard religious (Sharia) and legal rights
- Protect the human dignity of women
- Maintain the well-being of the family
- Fight customs, traditions, and practices that cause violence against women contrary to the principles of Islamic Sharia
- Protect women who are victims or at risk of violence
- Prevent violence against women
- Ensure public awareness and education on violence against women
- Punish perpetrators of violence against women.

The EVAW law lists twenty-two acts considered to constitute violence against women and covers physical, sexual, emotional and psychological abuse (e.g., beating, harassment), crimes related to marriage (e.g., child marriage, forced marriage), *baad*, deprivation of inheritance and property, and denial of access to education, work, and healthcare. Sections of the articles of EVAW (including articles on punishment of physical, sexual, and emotional abuse) can be found in Appendix A.

The EVAW law was passed by presidential decree in August 2009, but three years after its implementation only a small per centage of crimes against women were being followed up by the Afghanistan government. The Afghanistan Independent Human Rights Commission registered 2,299 incidents of violence against women between March 2010 and March 2011 that fell under the purview of EVAW. A UN study revealed that only 594 cases had been opened (26 per cent of the total cases filed). Indictments were filed only in 7 per cent of cases (155 cases), and the EVAW law was used to pass judgment in only four per cent of cases (101 cases).

Clearly, enacting the law to end violence against women is the right step forward, but the need to change people's mind-set is dire. According to a popular proverb in Afghanistan, "a woman's place is either her husband's house or her grave." A consistent way of educating and changing the way of thinking that is so deeply etched in the minds and hearts of Afghan people is a matter of paramount importance, especially regarding those who live in rural areas.

We must walk a long road before Afghan women are safe and protected. The UN report that was released on November 23, 2011, "A Long Way to Go: Implementation of the Elimination of Violence against Women law in Afghanistan," clearly noted that the Afghan government had not succeeded in applying the landmark EVAW law to the large number of cases of violence against women.

The UN High Commissioner for Human Rights, Navi Pillay, said:

> Judges, prosecutors and police in many parts of Afghanistan have begun to use the new law, which is a positive development, but unfortunately only in a small per centage of violence against women cases...Although the law's implementation is clearly growing, there is a very long way to go before Afghan women are fully protected from violence and their equality is properly upheld through this important law.[8]

The Director of Human Rights for the UN Assistance Mission in Afghanistan, Georgette Gangon, says:

> As long as women and girls are subject to violence with impunity that violates their human rights...Ensuring rights for Afghan women—such as their participation in public life, including in the peace and reconciliation process and equal opportunities in education and employment—requires not only legal safeguards on paper, but speedy and full enforcement of the EVAW law.

Some government officials and state mechanisms have started to waver in their stance on the protection of women's rights. The EVAW law was a product of four years of dialogue and negotiations with many sectors. It was enacted through a presidential decree in 2009 and has since been used in prosecuting violence-against-women offenders. Despite its validity and the adequacy of its coverage and punitive provisions, in May 2013, attempts to have it ratified by parliament caused an uproar. Following heated discussions, protests, demonstrations, and counterdemonstrations, the process stalled. In June 2013, a parliamentary committee was commissioned to review the EVAW law; it is yet to be ratified by the parliament. Fundamentalist solons have branded it as un-Islamic. One of them even warned that "there will be blood in the streets if the law will be enacted." Presently, the law is under threat of being amended or repealed. In addition, division among women's leaders is being fomented by the debates on the legality of the EVAW law. Amidst the heated controversies about the EVAW law, the Ministry of Women's Affairs, which is mandated to protect women's rights and mediate conflicting views from an enlightened perspective, was disappointingly silent. Strikingly, on many issues, the Ministry of Women's Affairs has constantly stood on the side of the government, even if its decisions are deleterious to women.

When approached by women activists for help in defending the EVAW law, President Hamid Karzai informed them that women's rights had already brought tremendous trouble and shame to his leadership and that he will no longer be able to extend any help.[9] This mindset is alarming, considering that he is the prime state official who is ultimately accountable for the protection of women's rights. In 2013, President Karzai appointed commissioners who lack knowledge and commitment to women's rights to the Afghanistan Independent Human Rights Commission. They include a hard-line fundamentalist and former member of the Taliban government, who was jailed in Bagram by American soldiers for his insurgent activities. He asserted that the EVAW law was un-Islamic and must be changed. Only under pressure from the Human Rights Watch and UN High Commissioner on Human Rights was the said Commissioner dismissed from office by the president.[10] Although this is a welcome development, it is also clear that President Karzai is inclined to sacrifice the interests of women to placate the Taliban. The rest of the new appointees to Afghanistan Independent Human Rights Commission have also questionable records on human rights. One of them, QadriaYazdanparast, was closely associated through Jamiat-i-Islami with Afghanistan's warlords, many of whom maintain private armies even while holding government posts.[11] It should be noted that the Civil Society and Human Rights Network submitted twenty-seven names for consideration by President Karzai but none of the bearers of those names was appointed.

Women's Employment in the Civil Service

The Karzai government appointed its first female provincial governor, Habibi Sorabi, in 2005, and Azra Jafari became the country's first female mayor in 2009. By 2011 there were about 1,195 women police officers. About 4 per cent of judicial officials in the country are women.

The government of Afghanistan and its Ministry of Women's Affairs presented its National Action Plan for the Women of Afghanistan in 2006. So far, there has been no follow-up progress report, much less any annual report on the achievements and challenges in implementing this plan.

Attacks on women have increased in recent times, despite President Karzai's public assurances. Amnesty International's 2011 Human Rights Report on Afghanistan states that although 1,891 cases of violence against women were documented in 2010, the true number may be much higher. Afghan women and female politicians have increasingly been attacked.

Member of Parliament Shukria Barakzai receives regular death threats for speaking out on women's issues. She is one of the most outspoken of Afghan parliamentarians and is often openly threatened with death in parliament.

Shinkai Karokhail, an outspoken member of parliament for Kabul, has been voicing concern about the Karzai government's decision to talk with the Taliban. She believes that women "must not be the sacrifice by which peace with the Taliban is made." Over the last few years, she has been issuing warnings on the implications of a deal with the Taliban. "We have to draw red lines for the Taliban," she said. "They have the right to be a participant in our system, but they must know that there are lines they cannot cross. The women of Afghanistan do not want to be forced back inside their homes again."[12]

Landmark Resolutions on Women, Peace, and Security

More than a decade after the UN Security Council adopted Resolution 1325[13] on women and peace and security on October 31, 2000, major gaps in the implementation of the resolution and a lack of accountability continue. The landmark resolution was unanimously adopted and reasserted the important role of women in postconflict negotiations, reconstruction, and peace building. Resolution 1325 urged governments to involve women in peace and security.

The unprecedented Resolution 1325 adopted under Chapter VI of the UN Charter is binding on all UN member states and has been reaffirmed by them, including the government of Karzai. The obligations are applicable to Afghanistan, and several of the mandate agreements signed by the Karzai government reaffirm the importance of Resolution 1325, the need to involve women in the peace process, and the promotion of women's rights in war zones. The resolution is an action document and is meant to be a framework for bringing women to the centre of the reconstruction and peace processes.

Thirteen years later, the Security Council unanimously reaffirmed the need for the consistent implementation of Resolution 1325 and the aim to strengthen women's roles in all stages of conflict prevention, transitional justice, rule of law, and reconstruction. With Resolution 2122[14] of October 18, 2013, women were guaranteed a seat at the peace table. Secretary-General Ban Ki-Moon noted that "[t]his is a matter of gender equality and human rights, and crucial to achieving sustainable peace, economic recovery, social cohesion and political legitimacy."[15] In addition, the UN High Commissioner for Human Rights Navanethem Pillay noted the need for full participation by women in context- and gender-specific transitional justice strategies. The text noted that women's rights were integral to the maintenance of international peace and security:

> Reaffirming that women's and girls' empowerment and gender equality are critical to efforts to maintain international peace and

security, and emphasizing that persisting barriers to full implementation of resolution 1325 (2000) will only be dismantled through dedicated commitment to women's empowerment, participation, and human rights, and through concerted leadership, consistent information and action, and support, to build women's engagement in all levels of decision-making.[16]

Obstacles to Education

Girls face many obstacles attending school and even put their lives at risk. In the eastern Kapisa province, schoolgirls have been shot by local Taliban members on their way home. As a woman and medical doctor, it pains me to hear stories like the one about Anisa. Anisa was a girl in grade 10 and worked as a volunteer in a polio campaign in Kapisa. She was returning home from the Mahmoud Raqi Girls High School when she was killed by a volley of bullets from armed men. Kapisa Head of Women's Affairs Saifoora Koohestani said local Taliban gunmen committed the deed, although the group has not claimed responsibility. The Taliban has opposed the polio campaign in parts of Pakistan and Afghanistan. Several instances of students being killed or attacked have taken place, but many incidents are not reported. In October 2012, Pakistani schoolgirl Malala Yousafzai received worldwide recognition after surviving being shot in the head by Taliban militants for her work in promoting education for women. The country has a 14 per cent female literacy rate—contrast this figure with a 99 per cent female literacy rate in the United Kingdom and the United States. In 2010, more than seventy-four schools, including twenty-six girls' schools and thirty-five mixed gender schools, were destroyed or closed on account of violence.

Among many other necessities of life, education is also denied women. Every effort to educate Afghanistan's women has been met with a counterforce of much greater intensity. No more is required of a woman than that she remain confined within the four walls of her house. Conditions worsened with the Taliban coming into power; before the Taliban, women were allowed to attend school and university, both to teach and to study.

From 1996 to 2001, educational institutions in Afghanistan fought for their survival as never before. Schools and universities were destroyed, while females were banned from even setting foot in educational institutions. Today, many Afghan families will permit their daughters to attend only allgirls schools close to home, while other families believe it is unnecessary for girls to be educated at all. Schools for girls have been burned down, teachers of girls have been threatened or killed in their hundreds, and schoolgirls have been physically harmed while walking to school.

Post-Taliban, a number of efforts aimed at reconstructing the shattered position of women in society have been made; however, the improvement is negligible. Nonetheless, the efforts that have been made in reinforcing women rights for education are commendable.

Many challenges face education in Afghanistan, including the lack of books, teachers, and security. In rural parts of the country, there are reports of students graduating from high school without even the ability to read or write properly. Much of the educational material during the Taliban period was influenced by the Taliban's religious leaders in Pakistan, where only religion was taught and women were forbidden to attend school. As we have seen, even after the fall of the Taliban, the Taliban continues to be active in the destruction of schools and the targeting of girls.

Efforts to improve the educational status of women in Afghanistan started soon after the fall of the Taliban. Immediately after the extremist group left the nation, the reconstruction of the education system became the top priority for human rights activists. Several projects were undertaken to facilitate women's education, with special emphasis on developing technical and managerial capacities of government and civil society.

In May 2012, more than 120 girls in the Bibi Hajera girls school were admitted to a hospital after being poisoned in their class in the provincial capital of Talokhan. According to a CNN report, the traumatized girls experienced symptoms including dizziness, vomiting, headaches, and loss of consciousness.

Police Spokesman Khalilullah Asser noted that the

> Afghan people know that the terrorists and the Taliban are doing these things to threaten girls and stop them going to school. That's

> something we and the people believe. Now we are implementing democracy in Afghanistan and we want girls to be educated, but the government's enemies don't want this.[17]

A September 2009 CARE report gives some extremely interesting and enlightening data regarding the education system in Afghanistan. The report, titled "Knowledge on Fire: Attacks on Education in Afghanistan," states that

> [t]hroughout 2008 alone, 670 attacks on the Afghan education system were carried out including arson and the murder of teachers and students. Between January 2006 and December 2008, 1153 attacks of different natures were reported: grenades, night letters or verbal threats to teachers, killings of students and education personnel.[18]

The report also notes that, according to the Ministry of Education, 230 people have died as a result of attacks on schools between 2006 and 2007. According to the UN Children's Fund (UNICEF), the most common attack on schools was arson.

The 2006 Human Rights Watch report "Lessons in Terror: Attacks on Education in Afghanistan" lists three different groups that are responsible for the attacks: (1) the armed opposition, (2) regional warlords and militia commanders not loyal to the central government, and (3) criminal groups, mostly involved in the narcotics trade.

In Afghanistan, girls are required by law to go to school; however, many of them never do. Death threats, acid attacks, and bombings by Taliban militants and other extremists force many parents who support female education to keep their daughters at home. Families who stand in the way intensify the problem. School officials in conservative communities say relatives are often more interested in marrying off their daughters or sisters than in helping them get an education.

But some girls, like eighteen-year-old Rahmaniya, are fighting back. The tenth grader in the southern city of Kandahar province says that the moments she savors most in her life are those she spends learning. Rahmaniya, whose last name is being withheld to protect her, says she did not dare go to school until her father passed away five years ago. He had vowed to disown her if she attempted to get an education.

These days, the slight girl with big brown eyes dreams of going to college to study journalism. But, she adds, it's hard to think about the future when her older brother keeps threatening to stab her to death with a knife he carries in his pocket. "Several times he has beaten me up," she says. "He tells me, 'You go ahead and go to school, and I'll throw acid on you like the Taliban. I'll go to the Taliban, and they'll protect me if I do this in this land of infidels where girls go to school.'"

Rahmaniya has been driven into hiding, and she believes her brother's anger is rooted in jealousy, since he quit school a long time ago. Her family, like many in Kandahar, is also struggling to make ends meet, and the teen says her brother wants her to marry. In Afghanistan, dowries bring in a lot of cash for the bride's family. "But I don't want to get married, at least not before I finish my studies," Rahmaniya says.

Her brother's insistence that she wed is something Rahmaniya uses against him. She explains that when he threatens to blind or maim her, she reminds him that disfiguring her will make it impossible to find a husband. Nevertheless, the threats and beatings have driven Rahmaniya into hiding. She moves every few days from one sympathetic relative's house to another to avoid being found by her brother.

Last week, her mother agreed to help plan her daughter's escape to a women's shelter in Kabul so that she could continue her studies in safety. The plan fell apart when Rahmaniya's mother caved into family pressure that her daughter marry a relative. The mother says the man will allow Rahmaniya to attend school after they wed.

Education is pivotal to the new vision of Afghanistan. If there is any country in the world whose need for non-stereotyped learning is most profound, that country is Afghanistan. Removing cultural, religious, and gender prejudices in the curricula and educational material is a strategic entry point towards a meaningful life. There are no available studies on the extent of religious and cultural prejudices in Afghan schools. With regard to gender, however, a study conducted in 2010 by Khalid Fahim, entitled "Gender Issues and Textbooks: Gender Bias in Phasto Primary School Textbooks in Afghanistan," showed that the roles that are depicted for women in our school textbooks continue to be stereotyped; women are less active than men, they do not make decisions, and they are confined to reproduction. Women are portrayed disproportionately less than men in the schoolbooks, and whenever they are depicted in the public sphere, they are shown in traditionally female roles, such as teachers and vaccinators. Concepts and languages are male centered, resulting in female invisibility in many subjects. Worse, school authorities and personnel believe that the roles of women as portrayed in school textbooks need to reflect the values of a conservative Islam society—an indication that Afghan schools serve the purpose of reproducing patriarchy, gender conservatism, and female marginalisation.

In the last decade, the removal of stereotypes in educational materials and curricula has received attention from certain donors, NGOs, and international organisations. However, such attention is too little to generate a transformative potential in society, particularly as regards the generations to come. Some essential requisites appear to have been missed, including the following:

Commitment to the principles of democracy and human rights. The elimination of prejudices in school curricula and learning materials must be predicated upon a strong commitment to the principles of democracy and human rights. Respect for rights and human life, equality, nondiscrimination, individual freedom, empowerment of the disadvantaged, tolerance, inclusiveness, and similar philosophies are vital to the framing of principles and initiatives that promote tolerance and impartiality in schools and in all aspects of life. The elimination of religious, cultural, and gender-based stereotypes in curricula and learning materials will have a stronger chance of being sustained if it is founded upon the commitment of school officials, personnel, students, parents, and citizens to democratic and human rights values, making the elimination of prejudice both a political and personal exercise. The eradication of prejudice cannot be a mere official task or responsibility of a handful of civil servants and professionals, who, after a while, may no longer be in the position to support nonstereotyping in the school system.

Comprehensive approach. As we have just noted, the elimination of stereotypes in school curricula and learning materials may never succeed if pursued as a stand-alone approach. Rather, it has to be positioned within a broad strategy to address the very roots of prejudices in all walks of life. This strategy requires collaborative efforts, especially among institutions that establish the framework for what is acceptable or not in a given society. Foremost among these, in Afghanistan, is the religious sector, which has a strong, commanding influence in the minds of people and on their behavior. Religious leaders should echo what the schools teach and vice versa; dissonance leads to confusion, tension, and struggle among institutions and people.

Thus, to be meaningful and sustainable, interventions to rid schools of stereotypes need to begin with multisectoral consensus; transformation can only occur at the broadest level. Collective commitments have to be generated, and responsibilities within all institutions have to be clarified, paid attention to, and supported.

A teacher-student partnership. Breaking away from stereotypes within school settings requires a solid teacher-student partnership. Teachers and students usually come to school with their own deep-seated stereotypes—learned through years of upbringing and socialisation by family, media, peers, and society. Because of these influences, the actual interactions between and among them are loaded with stereotypes that are not seen in curricula and learning materials. It is vital, therefore, for teachers to have the proper training to be able to deal with various manifestations of stereotypes as they arise in the school setting and classroom interactions. Training for this purpose has to be incorporated into teachers' education and refresher training curricula. Likewise, it is an imperative for students to acquire skills to identify and question stereotypes whenever and wherever they occur, regardless of whether they are exhibited by fellow students or by school authorities. Thus, teaching materials should incorporate practical exercises in actually detecting religious, cultural, and gender stereotypes, as well as skills in offering alternatives to such stereotypes.

Participatory monitoring of biases and stereotypes. Although certain state instrumentalities are given official responsibility to ensure that textbooks and school materials are free from cultural, religious, and gender stereotypes, this responsibility is actually shared by everybody. Parents, students, media, civic organisations, and other sectors of society must be encouraged to participate in ridding school materials and textbooks of such kinds of stereotypes through reporting, critiquing, and providing alternatives that will promote equality between girls and boys, women and men. Accessible mechanisms through which such sectors could coordinate and report on the presence of stereotypes in school materials, curricula, and practices must be set in place. Parents and teachers associations should consider including the elimination of prejudices in schools as one of their active areas of concern.

Ensuring consistency and harmony with actual practice. Freeing teaching materials and textbooks from stereotypes is in itself not enough. It is equally important for school institutions, authorities, and personnel to demonstrate their commitment against such stereotypes through policies, practices, statements, and activities. For example, schools should strive for at least 30 per cent representation of women to men in school decision making. School authorities should also constantly pronounce their commitment to eliminate stereotypes in schools and on campuses. Teaching practices, school infrastructures, languages, and everything else in the school must reflect the absence of religious, cultural, and gender stereotypes. Any message or act suggesting tolerance of violence against women must be nipped in the bud. No reaction would confuse the students and neutralise the impact of removing stereotypes from textbooks and school materials.

Simple guidelines and indicators could aid teachers to help students to determine religious, cultural, and gender stereotypes in teaching materials, curricula, and other school based events or activities. Examples of gender stereotypes are (1) the assignment of roles or responsibilities based on sex, (2) the exclusion of females or males from an activity on account of sex, and (3) discouraging girls or boys from making free choices and encouraging them to make choices based on what society dictates. A mechanism should also be designed to enable students and teachers to immediately report the continuing presence or practice of stereotypes in school lessons and activities.

All sexist and culturally offensive language should be removed, and some terminologies should be changed; for example, "mankind" should be replaced with "humankind." One could question the generic use of "he" and "him" that assumes the inclusion of females and the placement of male terms ahead of female terms at all times, such as "men and women" instead of "women and men" or "boys and girls" instead of "girls and boys." Language and mental images coexist; the constant placement of "boys and men" ahead of "girls and women" may well reinforce the subliminal message that men and boys are more important and should always come first.

Pictures should not depict women and girls or ethnic and religious groups in weak, subordinate, or traditional roles. Rather, they should be shown in empowered and nontraditional roles, such as decision makers and holders of nontraditional jobs (e.g., lawyers, doctors, engineers). They should not always be in the background, small and innocuous. Pictures commercializing women's bodies, depicting women as sex objects, or portraying them in abusive relationships should be altogether banned.

Songs and messages that affirm the traditional roles of women and men, and the inferiority of any person—male or female—or of any religious, ethnic, or cultural group should be replaced with messages that promote equality and non-stereotyping. Songs that romanticize emotional battering, martyrdom, or the suffering of women and other religious or cultural groups should be critiqued from an enlightened perspective and removed from curricula and teaching materials. These approaches should also be applied to jokes and other forms of written, verbal, and visual communications.

Games that reinforce sexual, ethnic, or religious stereotypes should be prohibited. The assignment of games or jobs at school should be based on the preferences and potential of individual students. Girls and minorities must be given coaching or leadership roles in sports teams and other extracurricular activities, and they should number no less than 30 per cent of the total. Sexual harassment committed against girls, women, and minorities must be eliminated.

Use of blue, green, and brown for boys and pink, yellow, and red for girls should be discouraged. The assignment of colors should be based on random choices or reasons other than their association with gender or religion. Selections of colors in school settings based on religious, cultural, or gender prescriptions should never be encouraged.

Lack of Access to Health

Childbirth is associated with further adversity: a woman dies every twentyseven minutes in Afghanistan due to pregnancy-related complications. There are on average 1,600 maternal deaths per 100,000 live births. But in the remote mountainous province of Badakhshan, the rate is 6,500 per 100,000—the highest recorded rate of maternal mortality in the world.

Like education, the health system in Afghanistan has suffered innumerable challenges for decades. Women are at a much higher risk of suffering mental and physical problems than men.

Decades of exposure to violence, aggression, and terror have left women with devastating psychological consequences. According to a 2001 WHO report, titled "Afghan Education for a Better Tomorrow," it is estimated that more than five million Afghan women and men suffer from various types of mental distresses, including posttraumatic stress disorder, depression, anxiety disorders, and substance abuse and dependence.

Various reports reveal a number of startling statistics relating to Afghan women's mental health conditions.[19] High suicide rates and selfimmolations among Afghan women and girls have dramatically increased. Treatment services for affective disorders, stress, and other psychological disabilities are few and far between. One report concludes that 98 per cent of Afghan women suffer from posttraumatic stress disorder. Mental health needs of Afghan women have not received adequate attention from the aid community and NGOs. There is an acute lack of services for people with learning disabilities. A lack of trained female rehabilitation workers makes treatment even less accessible to women, for whom cultural barriers prevent treatment by male workers. International and local programs addressing domestic violence are scarce. In particular, there are no known projects or programs at all in remote areas, where Afghan women are more vulnerable.

There is a high number of female drug users in Afghanistan, who often use opium to self-treat for trauma, insomnia, and other problems. Due to the stigmatisation of female drug users, they face barriers to treatment. Economic considerations and a lack of child care in rehabilitation facilities also prevent women from getting the mental health help they need.

Violence against women—physical, sexual, and psychological—is pervasive within Afghan society, affecting an overwhelming majority of women and girls. Violence against women and "honor" crimes are considered taboo subjects and thus are not widely reported to the police. There are estimates of as many as five thousand unreported cases a year; but in reality this number may be much higher. Typically, the violence is committed by males, mainly family members who often receive the indirect support of community leaders (Afghanistan Independent Human Rights Commission, 2006), or by other direct family members, sometimes female family members, and consistently by someone the victim knows.

The courts have many shortcomings, including too few well-trained judges and inadequate enforcement mechanisms, and as a result are not adequately protecting women under Afghan law. There are many cases of female victims who are unlikely to make it past the verdict rendered by local tribal councils. Afghan judges and court officials are likely to accept harm to women as a sentence befitting actions such as infidelity.

More recently, the World Health Organisation has made great efforts to restructure the health system in Afghanistan. A November 2011 report, "Improving the Health of Women and Children in

Afghanistan," notes the World Health Organisation's efforts in establishing training courses for midwives in Afghanistan and in working to improve the country's family planning services and to strengthen the capacity of health personnel to conduct reproductive health research. These initiatives are positive but have yet to yield large scale improvement in Afghan women's health.

The 2012 report "Afghan Reproductive Health Strategy Launched" by the Afghan Ministry of Public Health and the US Agency for International Development explained a four-year plan for reproductive health. According to the Minister of Public Health Dr Suraya Dalil's statement, this revised policy and strategy is designed to guide the Ministry of Public Health in addressing the reproductive needs of Afghanistan. The project's focus is on setting the right tone for donor countries and meeting their objectives as part of the Millennium Development Goals.

It is a vicious circle in Afghanistan, a vicious circle of poverty, lack of education, and no medical facilities for women. And so, no significant improvement to date has been possible to rectify the condition of women in society. The healthcare sector is governed by strict regulations stipulating that a woman cannot be examined by a male doctor. If there are no educated women in society, how is it possible to have female doctors in Afghanistan? I was fortunate to receive my medical degree before the Taliban took over. Post-Taliban, the doors of education opened up slowly for women; but they need to open even further, and women must be encouraged to go to the health sector.

Testimonies of Women's Abuse

In a land where a few decades ago even a woman's giggling was barred, today we can see a number of women speaking out against the wrong that has been done to them. True, it is likely too late now to provide justice to past sufferers; however, there is no denying that the harm that is not yet done can be nipped in the bud.

Women have to bear with injustice and violence to a far greater extent than men. Brutality prevails in the form of domestic violence, rape, forced marriage, and charges of adultery. The testimonies that follow about the many tortures inflicted upon the women in Afghanistan need to be published, however difficult it may be to read them. Without doubt, readers will be as outraged as I am every day when I hear these stories.

Lal Bibi

On May 17, 2012, Lal Bibi was abducted, chained to a wall, and raped and beaten over five days. The reason for her ordeal was the offense that her cousin had given to a family who had connections with the local militia commander. It was at his behest that she had been abducted, beaten, and raped.

Eighteen-year-old Lal Bibi did what is rarely seen in Afghanistan; she spoke out and publicly accused the local militiamen who had tormented her. Several of them happened to be members of the US-trained local Afghan police.

Normally, in such cases, the girl's family kills the girl since she is considered to have brought shame on the family; but in this particular case, Lal Bibi's relatives supported her and brought a badly battered and bruised Lal Bibi to Kunduz hospital, which was close to their home in northern Afghanistan. The family filed a complaint with the governor and hoped for justice; the alternative for Lal Bibi was death, which would be the only other way to restore the family honor.

Lal Bibi said as much in an interview, her voice shaky and painful: "I am already a dead person. If the people in government fail to bring these people to justice I am going to burn myself. I don't want to live with this stigma on my forehead. People will mock me if these men go unpunished, so I want every single one of them to be punished."

In a country where a woman is thrown into prison for having been raped on charges of moral crime, women like Lal Bibi are desperately needed to bring about a change. "She is very brave that she came out and talked to the media," said the head of the Afghan government's Women's Affairs Department in Kunduz. "She has set an example for the rest of the rape victims."

The prosecutor General Mohammed Sharif Safi said, "It is not the first time that they have committed such a horrible crime. All of them are a bunch of illiterate and uneducated bandits and thugs who go around harassing people." The provincial military prosecutors are looking into her case. Only two people have been arrested so far. One is the rapist Khudai Dad and the other is his brother Sakhi Dad, who is a member of the Afghan Local Police. The chief suspect in the Lal Bibi case is Commander Mohammad Ishaq Nezzami, who disappeared soon after Lal Bibi's abduction.

Lal Bibi had no clue as to what had conspired between her distant cousin Mohammad Issa and the family that sought vengeance in the shape of the Afghan Local Police commander, Mohammad Ishaq Nezzami. He barged into her house with a number of armed men, who grabbed her: "I was busy milking the sheep with my mother, and suddenly a car pulled up close to our tent…They first grabbed my father and tied his hands, and then the armed men grabbed me and my mother from behind, and I didn't know what happened and why they were there."

She was thrown into a truck and taken to Subcommander Sakhi Dad's home. It was his brother Khudai Dad whose daughter's honor had somehow been compromised by Lal Bibi's cousin. Lal Bibi can hardly contain her sobs as she narrates the story of how she was repeatedly raped by Khudai Dad and beaten by men. "I would begin to scream every time one of them came into the room, because I knew they were going to beat me or rape me again."

The Kunduz hospital report corroborates her story word by word: "The doctors found signs that she was beaten and tortured." The physical evidence confirmed that she had been chained. Since her hymen was broken during this ordeal, she is not fit to be married, because Afghan women are required to prove their virginity on the wedding night; if the test fails, they are often killed by the family in order to restore their honor.

Lal Bibi's mother and grandfather, too, are thinking of killing her if justice should fail to prevail. "If nobody wants to solve our problem, then they should behead her; we don't want her," said her mother. "Put yourself in our shoes: What if somebody raped your daughter? I am sure that when you see that no one is helping you to bring the culprits to justice, you will be ready to kill yourself, kill your daughter," says her grandfather, who has been by her side the whole time. "During the day, she sits and doesn't talk, and is silent for hours and suddenly she screams. Her soul has been broken, and she is a very sad person."

Lina

In early 2011, a young girl, Lina, was sentenced to death for possessing a cell phone. She was suspected of having been in touch with a boy on the phone. The girl was in her late teens and was accused of having dishonored her family. "My older brother took the cellphone from me and beat me very badly. It was dinnertime. They told me that they would execute me after dinner. They said to me this would be my last meal,"[20] said the girl as she narrated her story to the staff on the American military base where she had come to seek refuge:

> I was terrified to think of running away from home, but suddenly a voice from inside told me to flee before my brothers killed me. Maybe the devil made me do it…I took one of their cloaks and wrapped it around me to look like a man. Then I slipped out of the house and started walking to the foreigner's base nearby.

A community elder came and stayed with Lina at the base but stopped talking to her when she expressed her wish to remain with the foreigners. Her family pleaded for her to come home but she was still too frightened and refused.

Stories like Lina's usually end in the woman getting killed or burned in an acid attack. Lina was lucky enough to escape such a horrible fate. While Afghan officials agreed to look the other way, US officials flew her to a women's shelter in a large city. While appearing before an Afghan judge, Lina asked for help, and as he knew of a young Afghan man looking to get married, the two married. Marriage is the only way out for women.

Sahar Gul

Thirteen-year-old Sahar Gul was found imprisoned in her in-law's dark and dank cellar in Puli Khumri on December 27, 2011 by Baghlan province police. She had been living there seven months. Sahar had been a victim of forced marriage and was beaten and tortured violently by her husband and in-laws after she refused to work as a prostitute to earn money for her husband and his family.

She had multiple injuries on her body and was in a critical condition. She was suffering from head trauma and had a broken shoulder. Sahar had tried to flee her torturers but was sent back home by the local authorities. Several of her fingernails had been pulled with pliers, and one of her ears had been burned with an iron. Months after her forced return by the authorities the torture continued and came to an end only when a male relative paid her a visit and found her locked in the basement. She had been starved for weeks and was so weak that she was unable to speak. The details of how the community and authorities reacted to her ordeal have brought condemnation. Unfortunately, many people do not take this sort of crime seriously; even the senior advisor to the Ministry of Health, Abdul Fahim, called it the "bitter reality" of Afghanistan.

Estoray

This crime took place in Khanad, at a distance of fifty kilometers from Kunduz. Twenty-nine-year-old Sher Mohammad killed his wife for bearing him only female children. The couple had three daughters, the youngest of whom had been born three months prior. The Khanad district police chief, Sufi Habib, narrates that after the birth of the third daughter Mohammad started blaming his wife for not having a boy. The husband, with the help of his mother, first beat the woman and then strangled Estoray to death. After strangling and killing his wife, Mohammad ran away.

Mumtaz

Sixteen-year-old Mumtaz's face has been horribly disfigured with painful scars that stretch all across her face and body due to an acid attack. Acid was poured over her as well as her mother and sister because her father had refused her to a man ten years her senior. Two armed men held her head back as the man who had once asked for her hand poured acid all over her face.

Most of her body was burned. Some of the men involved in this heinous crime have been apprehended but the main culprit is still at large.

Peri

The women's shelters in Afghanistan help thousands of women victims; one of these women is sixteen-year-old Peri. She has brown eyes and a sad but pretty face. She narrates her horrific story in a detached manner. She was all of three years old when her father was accused of having killed a member of another family in her village. In a traditional settlement (baad), Peri was given to the victim's family as compensation. Though the tradition is illegal, it is nonetheless still common in Afghanistan.

At the age of ten, Peri was raped and was later forced to marry a boy belonging to the rapist's family. At the age of fourteen, she was drugged, beaten, and forced to marry another man. His other wife would threaten Peri at every moment. Peri had several attempts at committing suicide.

Serata

On July 3, 2012, Serata's ex-husband beheaded her and their two children, who were eight and nine years old. Their two-year-old daughter survived. Thirty-year-old Serata's killing is being called an honor killing. Serata had divorced her thirty-eight-year-old husband a year before her murder after having gone through a decade of domestic abuse. The police are still searching for him. In March and April 2012 alone, there have been sixteen reported cases of honor killings; many such killings take place but go unnoticed and unreported.

Aesha Mohammadzai

Aesha's story made international news. Aged twelve, she was offered to a Taliban fighter as compensation for a killing that was committed by a member of her family. She was married at fourteen, was abused constantly, and made to sleep in the stall with the animals. At eighteen, she fled her torturous life only to get caught by the Afghan police, who took her back to her captors. To avenge the dishonor that she had brought on their family by fleeing them, they decided to cut off her nose and ears. She was taken to the mountains, where her father in law, husband, and three other family members cut off her nose and ears and left her to die.

In an interview with CNN reporter Atia Abawi, she said: "When they cut off my nose and ears, I passed out. In the middle of the night it felt like there was cold water in my nose…I opened my eyes and I couldn't even see because of all the blood."[21]

She somehow managed to crawl to her grandfather's house, and her father brought her to an American medical facility, where she was looked after for almost ten weeks. She was then secretly moved to a women's shelter in Kabul and was then taken to America. There are hundreds, if not thousands, of women and girls that are tortured and killed in the name of culture, religion, and honor.

Samia

Samia was only seven years old when her horrible tale was told to the world in February 2006. Even a heart of stone would melt with one look at her frail figure, covered in scabs and scars. The patchy clump of hair on her scalp is probably due to the constant pulling of her hair by her tormentors. As you watch her speak softly in a recording that was made that year, you can hardly control your emotions. The worst part is that her story most probably is one of many.

Two years ago her father raped a ten-year-old daughter of a family in the Baghlan province of northern Afghanistan. Her father was arrested for the crime, and as per the popular and common custom of baad, he was asked to give his seven-year-old daughter to the father of the raped girl, Mohammad Yassin, to settle the case. Mohammad Yassin gave her to his son Omar Yassin in marriage.

Little Samia was taken to the Yassin household and kept there as a slave for two long and torturous years. She faced all sorts of tortures. The family locked her up in the basement and would beat her daily. She was burned with hot metal pieces, kept naked, left outside the house in the freezing cold for hours, and her hair were yanked every now and then. People of the area noticed her sad plight; when they could take no more, they forcefully entered the Yassin house. The locals removed her and placed her in the hands of security officials.

The cases have no end, and we have to face the fact that there are countless such cases that never get reported. The most probable cause of women not reporting such incidents and quietly tolerating all sorts of atrocities is that hardly any of them receive any kind of positive outcome or justice. It is no wonder that there is a high suicide rate among Afghan women; many are cases of self-immolation.

Saraya

In 2011, Saraya's story of escape from her torturous life was all over the internet as well as in the papers. She appeared on a television show, a brave act indeed for any Afghan woman.

She says, "I was forced to marry a rapist at fifteen. I ran away when I thought he would attack our daughter." She ran away for good. Despite her constant pleadings and begging, her father had not agreed to her not marrying a fifty-eight-year-old man. "I had so many dreams for my life," she said. "But when I saw him, they just disappeared. I told my father I didn't want to marry him. [I asked,] "Why are you doing this to me?" My father said: You're of an age to be married and this is my decision, not yours."[64]

She did not hold back with revealing the ill doings of her husband. She confessed that she believed that her husband would kill her as well as their children. She said on the television program Naqab, "When my youngest was just four years old, my husband brought women to the house and raped them. My child asked me, "Who are these women?" I could not say anything to my child; my husband would just beat me."

Zaynab

Zaynab (name changed to conceal identity) was forced by her father to marry an old man when she was eleven years old. Her husband treated her like a slave. Physical torture was a daily matter, and her husband even threw her out of a window. Zaynab ended her pain by running away from hospital and leaving her children behind. She said, "I put on men's clothes and a turban to hide my long hair and to look like a man, because it is extremely dangerous and difficult for women to travel by themselves."

Sahar Gul

Sahar Gul was beaten and tortured and had her fingernails ripped out after she was married off to a man almost twice her age when she was barely thirteen years old. Gul said that when she didn't conceive a child, her husband and his family started complaining that she was eating too much. They called her useless, stopped feeding her, locked her in a basement, and began torturing her.

Gul was not only tortured physically but was also harassed by her in-laws, who told her that since they wanted to purchase a new car, for which they required money, she should sell herself to other men.

Cases of Violence Against Women

The possibility that women's rights will be sacrificed in the name of peace is now a living reality. More than just making women's rights a bargaining chip, it is now clear that the peace and transition process is being used to justify the reimposition of fundamentalist tenets on women's oppression. The following data illustrate how the gains of the past ten years in women's rights are now being lost.

- The number of reported cases involving violence against women (VAW) increased from 2,299 to 4,010 for the period March 21 to October 21, 2012 compared to the number of cases for the same period in 2011.[22] This is a difference of 1,711—74.43 per cent higher than the original figure for 2011. Even if this is seen as an achievement in terms of peoples' willingness to report VAW incidents, it is still clear that (1) many women still suffer from violence, (2) offenders are not fully deterred by the presence of EVAW law because of its poor imple mentation, and (3) the need for response systems for VAW survivors is increasingly becoming a compelling imperative. Our fifty women's councils and NGOs scattered nationwide know for a fact that in their respective localities there are many more cases of VAW that are not being reported because of complicity by family members, lack of reporting mechanisms, and ignorance of the law and how it works.
- Increased incidents of brazen, extreme forms of VAW (i.e., mutilation, hanging, beheading, public execution) are now being reported more frequently in the media than previously. For example:

- In June 2012, Ministry of Women's Affairs Provincial Affairs Director Shah Jan Yazdan Parast reported to the media that eleven women had been executed by the Taliban in Parwan province alone during the preceding six months;
- The barbaric public execution of a twenty-two-year-old woman in Parwan was captured on amateur video and widely circulated in the media, obviously to sow fear in the hearts of women and to warn them of the return of a Taliban-style control of women;[23]
- On July 22, 2012, Radio Liberty reported that a man in Helmand Province shot dead his two teenage daughters, allegedly for being absent for four days;[24]
- Two women were beheaded by the Taliban in Kajaki District in Helmand Province in August 2012;[25]
- In October 2012, Mah Gul, a twenty-year-old woman from Herat, was beheaded by her husband's cousin and mother-in-law for refusing to prostitute herself.

The statistics are not being systematically recorded but poor records do not mean that the problem does not exist. Our partners in the field know the situation since they are part of the daily horrors routinely experienced by women at the hands of the Taliban and their own families and communities. As far as cruelty of women is concerned, it is "open season" once again in Afghanistan.

- The assassination of, and constant threats to, women defenders of human rights have been more rampant and brazen than before and have not received justice. For example:
  - Lieutenant Islam Bibi, commander of the Women's Police Department in the Province of Helmand, was killed on July 3, 2013, in Lashkarga City while on her way to her office;
  - In January 2013, the Taliban assassinated a female social activist in Wardak and hanged her dead body in a tree;

» On July 13, 2012, Hanifa Safi, the Head of the Women's Ministry, was assassinated in the province of Laghman by a car bomb;

» Najia Sidiqi, Acting Provincial Director of the Women's Affairs Department in Laghman, was assassinated on December 12, 2012;

» In September 2012, Kolsoom, a thirty-year-old woman from Herat Province, was stabbed to death by her husband, allegedly because she was working for an NGO development.

Notes

1. Poem by Dr Zieba Shorish-Shamley entitled *I Remember You.* Available at: http://www.afghan-web.com/woman/ziebapoem5.html
2. Afghanistan Independent Human Rights Commission 2011 report.
3. Available at www.rawa.org.
4. Quotes taken from Jalal Women News report, Mumbai, Hindustan Times, 2 December 2012.
5. "Gender–based Violence in Afghanistan," Afghan Women Network Report is available at: http://www.afghanwomennetwork.af/Gender%20based%20Violence%20in%20 Afghanistan.pdf
6. UN expert urges Pakistan, Afghanistan to ensure justice for recent killing of women, UN News Centre, 18 July 2012.
7. The Law on Elimination of Violence against Women (EVAW) enacted in 2009 is based on the Afghan Constitution and Islamic Sharia (EVAW law, Article 2).
8. *A Long Way to Go: Implementation of the Elimination of Violence against Women law in Afghanistan* at: http://unama.unmissions.org/Portals/UNAMA/human%20rights/November%2023_UNAMA-OHCHR-Joint-Report-on-Implementation-of-EVAWlaw_ENG.pd
9. This was relayed to Jalal Foundation by a woman activist who was present in the meeting with President Karzai.
10. http://www.hrw.org/news/2013/06/18/afghanistan-weak-appointments-underminerights- body.
11. "Critics Question Karzai Choices for Human Rights Panel," New York Times, Rod Nordland, 1 July 2013 at:

    http://www.nytimes.com/2013/07/02/world/asia/karzai-choices-for-afghan-humanrights- panel-raise-questions.html?smid=tw-share.
12. Arati R Jerath, "Lend them your ears," The Times of India, Crest Edition, 9 July 2011.

13. UN Security Council Resolution 1325 adopted at its 4213th meeting, on 31 October 2000.
14. UN Security Council Resolution 2122 adopted at its 7044th meeting, on 18 October 2013.
15. *Ibid.*
16. *Ibid.*
17. "Official: 122 girls, 3 teachers poisoned at Afghan school," Nick Paton Walsh, CNN, 23 May 2012 at:

    http://edition.cnn.com/2012/05/23/world/asia/afghanistan-girls-poisoned/index.html
18. "Who cares about the Afghan schoolgirls?" Lisa Lundquist, 2 September 2010. Available at: http://www.longwarjournal.org/threat-matrix/archives/2010/09/who_cares_ about_the_afghan_sch.php
19. Various testimonies of women in Afghanistan can be found at www.jalal-foundation.com
20. "Facing Death, Afghan Girl Runs To U.S. Military," Gale Global Issues in Context, 1 May 2012.
21. "The young woman who dared to defy the Taliban: Afghan, 22, rebuilding her life in the U.S. after having her nose hacked off in her homeland," Mail Online, 21 May 2101
22. Information received from office of the Afghanistan Independent Human Rights Commission, Kabul, 6 December 2012. See also *A Long Way to Go: Implementation of the Elimination of Violence against Women law in Afghanistan* at: http://unama. unmissions.org/Portals/UNAMA/human%20rights/November%2023_UNAMAOHCHR-Joint-Report-on Implementation-of-EVAW-law_ENG.pdf.
23. Jalal Foundation's compilation of news articles on Afghan women, volumes 1 to 9, 2012 to 2013.
24. Radio Free Europe/Radio Liberty, as compiled in Volume 2 of Jalal Foundation's Afghan Women News Digest, July 2012.

25 "Taliban behead 17 civilians, including women in Helmand for attending music event." RAWA.org, 27 August 2012. Available at:

http://www.rawa.org/temp/runews/2012/08/27/taliban-behead-17-civilians-includingwomen- in-helmand-for-attending-music-event.html

Chapter 3

Marriage Practices and Abuses

The extended family is integral to Afghan society, and marriage customs and practices are of enormous importance for both the country's social make-up and women. Although there are wide differences in marriage customs and practices across Afghanistan with its many ethnic and religious groups, what is common is the system of arranged marriages, wherein the parties involved enter into a formal agreement endorsed by their family members. Thus, marriage is a social contract and is bound by strict laws and restrictions. Moreover, most marriages are endogamous in that virtually all marriages take place within a tribal or ethnic group.

Marriage laws and practices are dictated by Islamic and tribal customs. Often these laws and customs do not respect religious or social diversity. For example, it is not possible for a non-Muslim man to marry a Muslim woman in Afghanistan, but it is possible for a Muslim man to marry a non-Muslim, foreign woman.

Moreover, Afghanistan, an Islamic republic, allows for polygyny under Sharia Law. Afghan men may take up to four wives, and though all wives are supposed to be treated equally, they rarely are. The practice of taking more than one wife, however, has become less and less prevalent in present times. Afghan courts will not register marriages involving Afghans who claim not to be Muslim, unless the couple consents to a Muslim religious ceremony. Afghan law considers all Afghans Muslim by default. If both or one of the parties are Muslim, the Family Court will register the marriage and perform the Muslim *nekah* ceremony. In addition, when a Muslim man wants to marry a foreign woman who is non-Muslim and the woman is not *kitabi* (of the book, i.e., Christian or Jewish), she must first convert to Islam.

In theory, women are protected by Islamic injunctions and given a dowry at the time of their marriage. This could be in the form of money or goods of some value. This dowry is meant for the woman's future in the case of divorce or the death of her husband. In practice, however, very few Afghan women are aware of this dowry system or what the money is meant for.

Forced Marriages

A daughter in a poverty-stricken Afghan household is often viewed as a burden and considered nonproductive because religion and tribal traditions bar her from most occupations. There is a tendency to get rid of female children through forced marriages even before the child attains puberty. The result is the perpetuation of a horrendous social malpractice—forced child marriage:

> In the rural areas of Afghanistan, girls are mostly married between ages of 7 to 11. It is really rare that a girl reaches the age of 16 and is not married. The customs, traditions and community they live in make it impossible for girls to break free from forced marriages.[1]

According to a UN report, between "60 to 80 per cent of marriages in Afghanistan are forced marriages." The report states that the reasons why girls are dragged into forced marriages are "repayment of debts; to solve a dispute and to pay family expenses."[2]

A report prepared by the Norwegian government stated:

> Even though the registration of births and marriages is highly incomplete in Afghanistan (Landinfo 2010), and other reliable data on marriages are unavailable, there can be no doubt that marriages involving very young girls (and boys) are prevalent in Afghanistan. According to the UN Children's Fund (UNICEF), a total of 57 per cent of all marriage agreements concluded in Afghanistan involve girls under 16 years of age (IRIN 2007). A study conducted in 2008 on the basis of approximately 200 marriages, shows that in more than 25 per cent of these marriages the age difference

between the spouses exceeded 16 years. Approximately 40 per cent of the marriages were agreed when the bride was 10–13 years old; in 32.5 per cent of the cases she was 14 years old, and in 27.5 per cent of the cases she was 15 years old (Women and Children Legal Research Foundation 2008).[3]

A recent report suggests that dozens of Afghan women kill themselves each year in order to avoid arranged marriages. The report narrated the story of a fifteen-year-old girl who was beheaded because she refused to get married. "Our investigation shows those who killed her were people who wanted to marry her,"[4] a Kunduz province police official told the BBC.

Up to 70 per cent of Afghanistan's seven hundred female prisoners are languishing in jails simply because they fled forced marriages or were victims of domestic violence, according to a Reuters report.[5] The same report quoted a Human Rights Watch statement, which said: "Now the onus is on President (Hamid) Karzai and his government to promptly free the women and girls who have lost months or years of their lives on these bogus charges." The Human Rights Watch statement came days after three senior Afghan officials—Justice Minister Habibullah Ghalib, Women's Affairs Minister Hassan Banoo Ghazanfar, and Deputy Interior Minister Baz Mohammad Yarmand—condemned charging women and girls for "running away" under the country's "moral crimes" law.

There are several reports of women who have been arrested and imprisoned due to false accusations by their neighbours. Women can spend years in cold prison cells without ever seeing their families. The case of Gulnaz, who spent years in an unheated Afghan prison cell with several other women and their children, made international news. Gulnaz was jailed for "moral crimes" because she was raped. Her child, who was a product of the rape, was in jail with her. She was accused of adultery while the rapist got no jail time. Had she decided to marry her rapist, she would have been released. Although the story brought a spotlight on the terrible conditions of human rights violations in our country, it is but one of many untold stories that I have heard during my many years fighting for women's equality.

According to UNICEF, 57 per cent of Afghan marriages involve girls under sixteen. Women's activists claim that up to 80 per cent of marriages in the country are either forced or arranged. And the problem is particularly acute in poverty-stricken rural areas. In these areas, many girls are forced into marriages when they are as young as nine or ten, says Khatema Mosleh of the Afghan Women's Network, a nonpartisan group of organisations that campaign for women's rights in Afghanistan. "Most marry far older men— some in their 60s—whom they meet for the first time at their wedding. So young are some girls", Mosleh says, "that they hold onto their toys during the wedding ceremony. And they usually become mothers in their early teens, while they are still children themselves."[6]

The Convention on the Rights of the Child and the Convention on the Elimination of All Forms of Discrimination against Women both condemn the deprival of girls' rights implicit in forced and early marriage. Afghanistan has signed these documents, and the Afghan Constitution states: "Any kind of discrimination and privilege among citizens of Afghanistan is forbidden. Citizens of Afghanistan, men and women, have equal rights and responsibilities in front of the law." "Despite these laws, only one out of five Afghan women possesses a national identification card, which makes it difficult for them to fully defend their rights."[7]

According to an October 8, 2003, study undertaken by the Institute of War and Peace Reporting, Afghanistan has one of the highest rates of widowhood worldwide. The International Organisation for Migration's Kabul office estimated the number of widows in Afghanistan to be over one million, and the United Nations Development Fund for Women placed the number of "war widows" in the country at more than two million in an April 11, 2006, report, with between thirty thousand to fifty thousand widows residing in the capital, Kabul. Most women are widowed as a result of the more than two decades of conflict in Afghanistan, during which many men were killed or went missing. Low life expectancy and early marriage in Afghanistan result in women often being widowed in their twenties and thirties.

The Supreme Court of Afghanistan has ruled that a woman can remarry if her first husband has been missing for more than four years and is presumed dead. Many Afghan women are not aware of the provisions of the law. Further, widows tend not to remarry since remarriage is generally considered taboo in Afghanistan.

According to the Representative of Widows for Peace and Democracy, women whose husbands have disappeared are highly vulnerable, since they are perceived to be neither widows nor wives. Because their husbands are missing but not officially deceased, these women are unable to claim their inheritance from the husband's family nor do they have the right to reside in the matrimonial home. Younger wives of men who have disappeared are vulnerable to sexual abuse, rape, forced pregnancy, and concubinage by the husband's family and others because they lack a male protector.[8]

Among the Pashtuns, widows are forced to marry the kin of the deceased—the brother of her deceased husband, in the first instance. However, in a non-Pashtun family, the girl is required to marry her brother-in-law to get support for her sister's children. Even worse, some sisters pay for their brothers' crimes by marrying the victims.

Fauzia Amini of the Women's Affairs Ministry says:

> The custom of forcing a widow to marry her brother-in-law or another close relative of her dead husband is very bad; we are trying to break the hold these traditions have on the population." The ministry is working with mullahs, or religious leaders, to try and get more freedom of choice for women whose husbands have died. Islam does not dictate that woman must marry within her husband's family, say religious scholars, such as Shaikh Zada, a mullah from Kabul province.[9]

The Pashtuns of Afghanistan also follow the system known as baad, which is a system of ending family feuds and enmities. When one Pashtun kills another, it signals the beginning of an endless round of vengeance killings and sometimes carries on through generations. To prevent such unending enmities, the Pashtuns have developed baad, where the victim's family approaches that of the murderer and demands compensation, which is usually a girl or two in marriage or sometimes property or cash. If an agreement is reached it signals the end of the feud but often condemns the girl to a forced marriage and a lifetime of oppression.

In northern Afghanistan and in other places where significant pockets of Shia Muslim communities exist, some reports suggest the fairly widespread and accepted custom of temporary marriage or *muta*. This is a marriage agreement of a specific, usually short duration of a night or a few months. Some claim *muta* is a veiled or socially acceptable form of prostitution. The Sunnis reject this Shi'ia tradition, and there is wide disagreement in Afghan society over this practice. Some claim that the *muta* was allowed by the Prophet Muhammad, while the Sunnis maintain that he later abolished the practice.

Shi'as constitute anywhere between 15 to 19 per cent of the population. They are mainly of the Twelver Shi'a and Ismaili sects. The Shi'as are generally an oppressed lot and include communities like the Hazaras, who were massacred by the Taliban in the thousands. Shi'as are mainly to be found in the western parts of the country around Herat, in Bamyan province, and in the north around Mazar-e-Sharif.

Perhaps the most abominable social practice that still exists in Afghanistan is *zina,* or extramarital or premarital sex. Under the Sharia, such acts are considered criminal and punishment is death by stoning. In Afghanistan most of the persons stoned to death for *zina* have been women. The Taliban used to make such occasions a public spectacle and organised gatherings to witness and participate in the unfortunate act. Afghanistan's civil code also outlaws sex outside of marriage and imposes heavy penalties and punishment for those found guilty.

During the time of Amir Abdur Rahman (1880–1901), a decree banned child marriages and forced marriages, and upheld the hereditary rights of women and their right to seek divorce. Of course, during the Taliban, all these rights were taken away. Although there has been some reform, I feel that all these efforts have, unfortunately, largely failed, and today the Afghan woman is more disadvantaged than ever.

Marriage and Sharia

I have spoken on several occasions on the plight of women in my country. Afghanistan still continues to treat women as second class citizens, and more women are being accused of adultery and dishonesty in marriage. In Afghanistan, women's lives are hanging by a thread; a woman never knows which neighbour will accuse her of adultery to seek revenge for an argument. Without any due process of the law, a women is left helpless. Some women have even been stoned to death because they were spotted alone in the market where they had come merely to purchase home groceries. A shadow of doubt is enough for a woman to be ridiculed, humiliated, abused, and accused by her husband of having no morals and character; as a consequence, many are abandoned by their husbands for dishonouring their family name.

Marriages in Afghanistan are principally based on the religious code of Sharia as well as the Afghan Civil Code of Conduct. Sharia applies to issues that are not considered within the civil code, and therefore marriage and many matrimonial norms of conduct are largely controlled by Sharia law.

In Afghanistan arranged marriage is the norm. Some girls are wedded off as early as age twelve, even though Afghanistan's marriage law stipulates that the minimum marriage age for a girl is sixteen years and for a boy, eighteen. However, underage girls can marry with the consent of their parents, which is why the law is open to interpretation. Most girls are not consulted on the matter of their own marriage, contrary to Afghanistan's Law on the Elimination of Violence against Women.

Under Sharia "temporary marriages" are promoted as an alternative to young people having extramarital affairs. As for a divorced woman, she cannot remarry the same man until she has consummated a marriage with someone else. However, a man who remarries the woman whom he divorced is not required to consummate a marriage with another woman. Even though both men and women can claim a divorce, men can do so more easily.

Shia Personal Status Law

When the Shia Family Law or Personal Status Law was adopted in February 2009, it made international news. The original intent was to give some recognition to the Shia minority. However, after consultation with the male Shia leadership, some pernicious articles were introduced to the legislation. Thus, Article 132 requires a wife to submit to her husband's sexual advances every four days. She can be denied food if she does not comply. Karzai tried to quietly pass the law, even with the heinous provision of denying women sustenance if they refuse to obey their husbands' sexual demands. The law also stated that a woman could not leave the house without her husband's permission. The law was only to affect Shia women, but all women knew that this move was an attack on all Afghan women. In attempting to pass the law, President Karzai was hoping to appease and earn favors from the Shia community.

Fortunately, many women activists, especially in the West, protested. Even Barack Obama called the clauses abhorrent. Political pressure and international outrage over the legislation persuaded Karzai's government to make some changes to the law, even though Karzai continued to claim in the international media that the law was not punitive to women. But the legislation improved only modestly. Most of the arguments that we put forward to parliament were ignored, and some of the most repressive provisions remain in the act. Women knew where they stood with the Taliban; Karzai's stance is frequently unpredictable. The Shia male leadership are strong supporters of the law and blame the West for interference in what they consider domestic affairs. Shia fundamentalist clerics argue that the law is a matter of national sovereignty.

Most Islamic law experts and human rights activists say that although the language of the original law has been changed, many of the provisions that alarmed women's rights groups remain, including Article 132. If any of the provisions are not followed by the wife, she is considered disobedient. The law was backed by the hardliner Shia cleric Ayatollah Mohseni, who is thought to have influence over the voting intentions of some of the country's 20 per cent Shia population in our country.

Notes

1. Forced Marriages in Afghanistan, Tahera Nassrat, Foreign Policy Association, 6 April 2010
2. *Ibid.*
3. Report Afghanistan: Marriage, LANDINFO, 19 May 2011.

4. 15-Year-Old Afghan Girl Beheaded For Rejecting Marriage Proposal. 29 November 2012. CBSDC.
5. Free jailed Afghan women fleeing forced marriages: group, Reuters, Nita Bhalla, 19 September 2012.
6. Afghanistan: Marriage Practice Victimizes Young Girls, Society, Farangis Najibullah, Radio Free Europe, 4 January 2008.
7. Forced and early marriages still common for girls in Afghanistan, Cornelia Walther, UNICEF, 17 March 2010.
8. Widows for Peace and Democracy, an Internet-based network of widow's rights organisations in England, 21 June 2006.
9. Afghanistan: Widows denied right to re-marry, Afghan Recovery Report, 31 January 2005.

Chapter 4

Burqa and Chador

The rulers came and went; however, the *burqa* survived. In fact, it has been there for so long that it has become part of the Afghan woman's identity. Without it she cannot step out of her house or be present among men in public. It is not easy for a woman to survive without the burqa in a nation like Afghanistan. Paradoxically, it is the burqa that is responsible for the social suffocation that women face in Afghanistan. The burqa propagates women's inequality and their dominance by men in society, which has, in turn, bred a fear in women that they will never be accepted as being of equal worth and value to the nation.

The History of the Burqa

The burqa is an assemblage of three garments: a small cap, a large cape, and a face veil. Also known as the chador (in Afghanistan), this garment covers the women from head to toe. The earliest references to this garment are in Indian Mughal paintings—the reason why it is commonly believed that the word burqa came to be used only after the coming of Taliban in Afghanistan; however, this commonly held belief is not true. The two terms, burqa and chador, have been used in Afghanistan for a very long time.

Constructed from around ten yards of fabric, the traditional Islamic burqa is a prerequisite for every woman. Be it a five-year-old girl or a seventyfive- year-old woman, concealment of one's self in this "conservative" garment has been an absolute must. An embroidered mesh face piece is used to cover the entire face of the wearer to allow her to breath.

The Significance of the Chador/Chadari

The chador, or *chadari*, is considered to be a nomadic woman's garment. The word chadari has been derived from the Persian word chador, which means tent. Women wearing a chadari are said to show respect towards the nation and the norms of the society. It is a symbol of respectability and honour for her as well as her entire family.

Apart from protecting women from pollution, dirt, and sand, it guards her—so men say—from their preying eyes. Until the Taliban, the chador and the burqa were viewed (mainly in the countryside) as protective attire for women. However, with the coming of the Taliban, the significance of this clothing altered altogether; the chador became stifling, a symbol of the increasingly aggressive social strangulation of women in Afghanistan. In the late 20th century, the garment was declared an Islamic requirement; but this new rule was not accepted by everyone. Conservatives in Afghanistan stepped up the punishment for women who stepped out without a burqa from a beating to the death penalty.

Sharia Law

Literally, the word Sharia means "the path to a watering hole." Being a religious code of conduct in Afghanistan, the Sharia is the foundation for Afghan society's beliefs and values. Sharia law has been adopted by a number of countries. Its strictness and implementation varies from country to country. The more the government demands adherence to Sharia, the more frequently are the stricter provisions enforced—and the greater the negative consequences for women.

It is believed that two original founders of Sharia law were Malik ibn Anas and Ibn al-Shaf'i. Anas established the Maliki school of jurisprudence and Al-Shaf'i was one of Anas' students; he disagreed with his teacher about the reliability of the hadith. Al-Shaf'I felt that it was necessary to trace each hadith from the time of Muhammad through its chain of devout Muslims. This concern led Islamic scholars to consider which hadith were true and which were not. Needless to say, these determinations have led to conflicts among scholars even to this day about the proper application of Sharia law.

The field of Sharia law is complex, and I must confess that I am not an expert. What is certain is that Sharia is widely misused; many Afghan leaders have an extremist take on this religious law, which has the consequence of threatening women's freedom and weakening any constitutional gains that are made by women.

I do not take issue with those Muslims who believe that Sharia originated in the words of Allah and in traditions that have their roots in the life of Prophet Muhammad. My concern is with the changing nature of Sharia and the way it is applied in our society today. Sharia is best defined as a way of life comprising legal, moral, and religious systems—all in one. It is this type of all-encompassing control over women that greatly concerns me, for who interprets Sharia but men and only men?

In Saudi Arabia, where Islam began, the strict interpretation of Sharia means that women cannot even drive a car or vote. It is believed that there are four schools of Sharia Law; namely, Hanbali, Hanifi, Maliki, and Shafi'i. Application of Sharia law varies between the four schools, which differ to a large extent from one another. Most Sharia apologists contend that the misuse or misinterpretation of Sharia is the problem. But is Sharia compatible with international human rights norms and the equality of men and women? I pose this question to those apologists. Very few of them speak out when women are being stoned and when hands are being cut off.

Under Sharia's civil code, a woman's testimony is worth half a man's. A man can divorce his wife by repudiation, whereas a woman must give justifications, many of which are difficult to prove. Child custody reverts to the father at a preset age; women who remarry lose custody of their children even before then. Sons inherit twice the share of daughters. Women at risk of domestic violence are put in further danger. In one study, four out of ten women attending Sharia courts were party to civil injunctions against their husbands.

Justice in Islam prevails in, and is guided by, Sharia Law. All of us in the Islamic Republic of Afghanistan are by law required to be

Muslims and to believe that it was Allah who revealed the Sharia Law. Violate Sharia, and you violate God. Sharia law uses gender differences to assign different and unequal rights to men and women in society.

The Rise of Fundamentalism

The Afghan fundamentalist (Islamist) movement has been active in Afghan politics since the late 1960s.[1] Its power and influence over the lives of Afghans were dramatically heightened by the sensational victory of Mujahideen forces over the Red Army during the Russian invasion of Afghanistan. At the time, the Mujahideen was strongly supported and armed by Pakistan and the United States. The main strength of this movement lies in its military power and political organisation. Although the movement is not united under a single leader, each of its factions exerts considerable influence on the lives of Afghans through engagement in various democratic activities, militant/terroristic actions, political affairs, religious worship, and the dayto- day activities of the people.

The main manifestation of fundamentalism is "radical Islam,"

which provides the ideological basis for a vision of Afghan solidarity as a nation. Unfortunately, this fundamentalism and "radical Islam" is totally averse to women's rights, feminism or gender equality. This ideology does not recognize women as equal human beings, it denies women their basic Human Rights and legitimizes the use of violence to sustain patriarchy and women's subordination. Female oppression and control is a sub-ideology of fundamentalism, something that came into full fruition during the rule of the Taliban. The truth, however, is that a sub-ideology of female oppression/control has been deeply embedded into the fabric of social institutions and the mindset of men, leaders and even many women. In other words, it is an ideology that is embraced not only by the Taliban but by many institutions and citizens of Afghanistan.[2]

The international intervention that began after the fall of the Taliban in 2001 endeavored to counteract female oppression by enshrining women's rights in the Constitution, adopting strategic policies to advance women's status, building their capacities, and promoting their participation in all walks of life. Unfortunately, as I noted previously, these gains are now under threat of being clawed back as fundamentalism reappears in formal and informal decision making—in the government, religion, families, and the community. Fundamentalism is a hibernating monster that has been reawakened by the announcement of the international community's imminent departure at the end of 2014.

Notes

1. Graham Fuller, *Islamic Fundamentalism in Afghanistan: It's Character and Prospects,* 1991.
2. Helena Derwash, "Afghanistan, my motherland," The Kashmir Walla, 23 October 2013.

Chapter 5

The Taliban's Ongoing War on Women

They made me invisible, shrouded and non-being
A shadow, no existence, made silent and unseeing
Denied of freedom, confined to my cage
Tell me how to handle my anger and my rage?[1]

This verse is from a poem written by the Head of Women's Alliance for Peace and Human Rights in Afghanistan. Zieba Shorish-Shamley aptly expresses the anguish and helplessness that is the fate of large number of Afghan women. The poem was published on the fiftieth anniversary of the United Nations Universal Declaration of Human Rights.

The very mention of the words equality and women's rights can ignite passion in my country from both men and women. Family pressures and customs, both old and new (introduced by the Taliban), and years of systematic gender discrimination have pushed Afghan women to the very brink of misery. I'm often asked why women do not fight for their rights. Life in Afghanistan is harsh, and most women are preoccupied with how to feed themselves and their families. Such is the reality.

Since the days of the Taliban, women have been denied an education and the right to work. They have been denied a voice or a choice in any and every area of their lives. Their continued struggle to make life livable is remarkable, by any standard. The overwhelming fear today is the rise—once again—of the fundamentalists and their desire to take over the country.

In July 2012, a three-minute Youtube video called "Taliban Kill Afghan Woman Accused of Adultery" made international news and was met swiftly with international condemnation. Karzai's government condemned the video in order to appease the international community. Each time such an incident takes place, the same sentiments are expressed, but sadly little else is done to change the situation.

The video is graphic, and it is alleged that it was the murdered woman's husband, with the authority of the Taliban, who shot the defenseless women five times at point blank range while a crowd of one hundred men looked on and cheered. The killing took place in a small town one hour outside of Kabul. The woman captured in the video kneels in the dirt and is covered in a burka. She makes no sound as the loud gun fire is heard. Women have no voice in Afghanistan; the Taliban have made sure of this. Men shout out that "Allah warns us not to get close to adultery because it's the wrong way." The government blamed the incident on a dispute between two Taliban commanders allegedly involved with the same woman.

This murder in cold blood has emboldened us to further action; however, many of our sisters in Afghanistan are scared to act. Such cowardly acts by the fundamentalists and their supporters must always be condemned. The government must pause to consider whether these tribal leaders be partners and destroyers of human rights and human dignity at one and the same time. The US government also condemned the murder but has done nothing to put pressure on the Afghan government to stop this criminal behavior.

It would be wrong to assume that the Taliban alone are responsible for such barbaric practices; in fact, these practices have existed all over Afghanistan. Honor killings are frequent, with men getting away with impunity.

Years after the fall of the Taliban from power, Afghan women are still being captured and put in jail for running away from their rapists and abusive husbands. Human Rights Watch published a 120-page report in March 2012, which describes young girls being forced to marry, being beaten viciously by their husbands, and threatened with death. Girls as young as fourteen have been forced into prostitution and subsequently been arrested for having been raped.

I myself have heard firsthand accounts of women who have been arrested for having run away from their abusive husbands—women who are terribly beaten, burned, whipped, and strangled almost to death. I invited one of these women to speak in my office during the June 2010 visit of Member of Parliament Mario Silva and Reverend Majed El Shafie from Onefreeworld International. The delegation that accompanied Reverend El Shafie was shocked to hear the horrific experiences of these women.

The Afghan government's growing aspiration to bring the Taliban to the negotiation table will inevitably be disastrous for women and for my country. Most of us cannot contemplate the possibility of being sent to prison for refusing to marry one's rapist, of running away from an abusive husband, of asking our husbands' permission to leave home. But that is the lot that Afghan women have to contend with.

It is estimated that there are 920 women in prison Afghanistan. Of these, 760 are in the age group of twelve to seventeen. In addition, there are 291 children, primarily as a result of what is termed "moral crimes." The Sharia system gives the rights to the men and the local committee of elders. The *jirga* sits as both the judge and jury and interprets Islamic law as they wish. In the case of Afghan women, this usually means being shamed in front of the entire community along with their children and getting sentenced to prison or death.

The injustice, the psychological harassment, the inequality and violence against women are a part of both the private and public lives of women in Afghanistan.

The overall statistics related to women and their general conditions are grim, with women suffering multiple forms of violence. Now, there is growing alarm over the number of women attempting to commit suicide. I have heard many of my colleagues who work at the hospital speaking of women attempting to kill themselves.

Most reports on the abuse of women note that the violence is never restricted to a single act of violence but rather involves a series of acts. The reports reveal that nearly two-thirds of Afghan women experience multiple forms of violence. But sadly, more than half of these crimes are not reported nor do women believe that they will receive justice.

In the case where domestic abuse is taking place in the home of the in-law family, it is often the mother-in-law who condones and instigates the violent acts and encourages the husband to use physical force to discipline his wife.

There are plenty of barbaric cases of husbands and family members violently penetrating the women with sticks as a punishment for shaming the husband. The severe bleeding from the assault ends in near death.

Less than 20 per cent of women know that other women are getting beaten by their husbands, which shows how most women are isolated in their suffering and pain. In urban areas, the stronger presence of government law enforcement bodies means that cases involving abusive husbands are less frequent than in rural areas, where women tend to suffer much more for the simple reason that they are at the mercy of local communities and their justice system.

Many women are outraged and frustrated with the state of affairs regarding gender inequality. Many of us want to bring about an end to the struggle and strife that is the lot of women's daily life. We want to change the way women are regarded and seen as the property of the men in the family.

Afghan women have very little say in the matters of home, community, or nation and are treated as pieces of property. According to tradition, the women must carry the family honor, which becomes a curse and no "honor." This curse puts any number of constraints on women's movements and interactions with the outside world. Very strict rules are in place when it comes to interaction with men. Only virgins can marry, and it is the possibility of the loss of virginity that pressures parents into marrying their daughters at an early age.

As noted above, extra marital sex (*zina*) is prohibited both by statutory and customary law. *Zina* is a part of the Sharia system, under which everything is based on eyewitness testimony. Unless four men appear as witnesses of the rape, the woman's narrative is not given any value. In the absence of male witnesses, a woman's accusations of rape are actually considered to be confessions of adultery. In these situations the woman is either stoned to death or put in prison.

A famous case in point is that of Gulnaz, who was convicted of adultery for being raped and falling pregnant by the rapist in 2009. Gulnaz was all of nineteen years when she was raped by her cousin's husband. Recalling the day when her life changed for the worst, she says, "He had filthy clothes on as he does metal and construction work. When my mother went out, he came into my house and he closed doors and windows. I started screaming, but he shut me up by putting his hands on my mouth."[2]

Gulnaz, like so many rape victims, was scared, knowing what would befall her if she were to tell anyone of what had happened. She tried to hide the incident for as long as she could. But when she started showing signs of morning sickness, she and her attacker were both arrested and charged with the crime of sex outside of marriage. When she made her appeal against the two-year verdict that was handed down, the court changed the decision to twelve years instead. She gave birth to her baby daughter inside Kabul's Badam Bagh jail. Many women have been killed after it was discovered that they were raped. Unfortunately, a woman's choice is stark; the only way to remove the dishonor of rape, to restore her family's name, and to have life beyond prison walls is for her to marry her rapist.

International pressure eventually persuaded President Hamid Karzai to "pardon" her; the victim had become the villain. From her prison cell, Gulnaz stated that she never imagined that she would have a daughter this way and that despite people telling her to hand her daughter over, she refused as a way of keeping the proof of her innocence. Her rapist had been serving his sentence in a separate jail and denied having raped her, yet agreed that she would be an open target for her family if she got out of jail. They would most certainly kill her to preserve their family name.

Most Afghan women who are convicted of *zina* are actually guilty only of fleeing a forced marriage or a violent husband and in-laws. Many who go to seek help from the local police end up behind bars. In cases of rape, the focal point in the eyes of the male-dominated Afghan society is not the rape but the dishonor that the raped victim is perceived to have brought to the family in the shape of what is considered to be her sexual immorality. *Zina bil Jabr* literally means "consensual extra marital sex by force" and has destroyed the lives of many Afghan women because of its legal implications.

Many Muslim women have raised this issue and pointed to the stark negligence of Afghan officials while prosecuting similar rape cases. Victims of rape and violence often suffer beatings in spite of laws having been enacted to safeguard them. Out of 2,299 cases of violence against women, indictments were filed for just 155.3 Women activists accuse the Karzai government of acquiescing—in the shadow of the imminent departure of the US and NATO troops in 2014—to pressure from fundamentalist elements in order to appease and maintain good relations with them.

Case Studies Since the Fall of the Taliban

June 26, 2004: Two women are killed and thirteen wounded from a bomb exploding on a bus carrying female election workers on their way to register women voters.

May 18, 2005: Shaima Rezayee, host of an MTV style music show, is shot in the head in her Kabul home.

June 23, 2005: A girl's school south of Kabul is set on fire by armed men.

July 3, 2006: Eight Female college students are wounded in an explosion in a women's English class at Herat University.

Sept. 25, 2006: Safia Ama Jan, the head of Kandahar's Women's Affairs Department, is shot and killed while walking to her office. She had been a teacher for three decades who fought for women's rights. During the Taliban rule she ran an underground school for girls.

Dec. 9, 2006: Two female teachers, who were sisters, and three other family members are shot and killed in their home by Taliban militants; twenty female teachers had been murdered up to that point.

May 21, 2007: Minister for Parliament Malalai Joya is ousted from the lower house for comparing the war lords to a stable of animals. She cannot keep track of the death threats she has received since her first speech to the council in 2003. She has survived four assassination attempts. Her situation is rare in that she actually has some security and bodyguards to help protect her.

June 1, 2007: Shakiba Sanga Amaaj, newscaster for Shamdhad, a private television network, is gunned down inside her house in Kabul.[4]

June 6, 2007: Zakia Zaki, journalist, owner and manager of Peace Radio, is gunned down inside her house in front of her eight-year-old son. She had been critical of the warlords.

June 26, 2007: Farida Nekzad, editor of independent news agency Pajhwok, receives death threats over her cell phone while she attends Zakia Zaki's funeral.

April, 2008: Grenades are thrown into the Herat home of radio talk show host Khadija Ahad.

May 15, 2008: Nelofar Habibi, television presenter in Herat, is dragged into a car and cut several times on the arm by a razor blade. Her male attackers tell her that she will be killed if she doesn't quit her job. She was previously stabbed in the abdomen in her home.

June, 2008: Bibi Hoor, a policewoman, is gunned down by men on motorcycles in Herat. She is the first policewoman to be assassinated.

July 14, 2008: Two women in blue burqas are shot and killed by Taliban outside Ghazni city; they were accused of running a prostitution ring.

September 21, 2008: Malalai Kakar, Afghanistan's most senior female police officer, is gunned down by Taliban on motorcycles while in her car in Kandahar; her son, who was her driver, is critically injured in the ambush. She had been receiving death threats for over a year.

October 13, 2008: A man murders his eighteen-year-old daughter-in-law with seven blows of an axe in front of her family when she refuses to return to her husband after visiting her family for *Eid*. The head of Women's Affairs for Samangan, Hanisha Afna, has urged punishment for the crime, which could be considered an "honor killing."

Children as Suicide Bombers

There has been an alarming increase in recent months in suicide bombings and attempted suicide bombings by children. Children as young as seven have reported that they were deployed as suicide bombers. Surviving children who trained as suicide bombers describe having been given amulets containing verses from the Quran that they were told would protect them from explosions.

Incidents in 2011 related to suicide bombings involving children include the following:

- On April 13, in Kunar province, an explosive vest detonated by a thirteen-year-old boy killed ten people, including five schoolboys.5
- In early May, five children, all under the age of thirteen, from Logar and Ghazni provinces, who had allegedly been trained as suicide bombers, were arrested by the National Directorate of Security.
- On May 1, a twelve-year-old boy blew himself up in a bazaar in the

  Barmal district of eastern Paktika province, killing four civilians and wounding twelve others.
- Around May 3, a fourteen-year-old boy, who said he had been coerced by the Taliban into carrying a bomb under threat that he would otherwise have his hand cut off, surrendered to international troops in Ghazni province.
- On May 20, in Nuristan province, a suicide vest strapped to a twelveyear- old boy exploded prematurely, killing several suspected insurgents, including the boy.

On June 26, an eight-year-old girl was killed in central Uruzgan province when a bag of explosives that the Taliban had instructed her to carry to a police checkpoint detonated. The Taliban's use of children as suicide bombers directly contravenes many of their public statements to the contrary. The recent announcements about the release of Taliban fighters from jail are further cause for concern; releasing them will only help strengthen the insurgency. We are, unfortunately, a country still at war, were the Taliban uses children as weapons. In 2012, the

National Front opposition party leader, Ahmad Zia Massoud, said that releasing insurgents from Afghanistan's prisons means strengthening the Taliban's "trenches." Massoud spoke at a "Woman's Rights in Society" conference in Kabul and noted that the recent government move to release seventy-nine suspected insurgents from two prisons would only lead to great insecurity in the country.

Notes

1. Zieba Shorish-Shamley, from "Look into my World" published on the 50th anniversary of the United Nations Universal Declaration of Human Rights.
2. "Afghan woman's choice: 12 years in jail or marry her rapist and risk death," Nick Paton Walsh and Masoud Popalza, CNN, 22 November 2011. Available at: http:// edition.cnn.com/2011/11/22/world/asia/afghanistan-rape/
3. "Implementation of the Elimination of Violence Against Women Law in Afghanistan has a long way to go." Joint report by the UN Assistance Mission to Afghanistan and the UN Human Rights Office, 23 November 2011. Available at: http://www.ohchr. org/EN/NewsEvents/Pages/Display News.aspx?NewsID=11635&LangID=E.
4. For more information see United States State Department 2008 Human Rights Report on Afghanistan.
5. "Afghanistan: Taliban Should Stop Using Children as Suicide Bombers, Human Rights Watch, 15 August 2011.

Chapter 6

Towards Enduring Peace, Democracy and Gender Equality

The implementation of a peace strategy will not be easy, but it is necessary. Flawed as it may be, the strategy, supported by the international community, is currently in place; there is no better option at hand. Despite the exclusion of many sectors, Afghans need to stand as a united nation and support our government to give the peace strategy a chance to succeed.

It might be of interest that there are currently several initiatives in support of this strategy. The Afghanistan Peace and Reintegration Program reported that as of January 2012, it had already enrolled 3,354 ex-combatants and has 442 new cases that have yet to be processed. The Afghan government also announced that in accordance with the second component of its strategy, fifteen individual Taliban have been delisted from the roster of officially recognised international terrorists.1

It is also noteworthy that as of January 2012, some US$157.5 million has reportedly been deposited in the Afghanistan Reconstruction Trust Fund to support projects that include small livelihood grants to ex-combatants. Community-based policing is also being strengthened, with eleven thousand members having been recruited to serve as community police in fifty-seven localities to date. Likewise, a United Nations Development Programme survey showed a 46 per cent improvement in the public perception of the police force, compared to

34 per cent in 2009. In addition, both the army and the police are reportedly on track in reaching their respective growth targets of one hundred and ninety-five thousand and one hundred and fifty-two thousand members respectively in 2012.

Within the South Asian region, President Karzai has received political support for an Afghan-owned, Afghan-led peace process, notably from the presidents of Pakistan and Iran. During the NATO summit in Chicago, he signed a framework for Afghanistan's security transition beyond 2014, which embodies a written commitment from NATO and the international community to continue their support for Afghanistan's peace and development initiatives, albeit on a bilateral basis.

Yet, some of our president's pronouncements and political actions confuse ordinary citizens and make them wary. For example, he announced that he is already engaged in peace talks with the Taliban, but the veracity of this claim was vehemently denied in the media by Taliban leaders. Likewise, to the great concern of the Afghan population, he declared that he supports the establishment of a Taliban office in Qatar to enable the Taliban "to come to an understanding with other nations." The wisdom of supporting an office for the Taliban, whether in Afghanistan or abroad is, at the very least, questionable.

Sadly, it was not until December 2011 that women were involved in the Bonn Conference on negotiations of the future of Afghanistan, and then only at the margins. Since the first Bonn Conference was held, Afghan women in a civil society remains the most significant debate in the context Afghanistan's development as a nation—but without any women present at the negotiating table.

Building Sustainable Peace

Amidst such developments, not only were women's perspectives ignored but the women's rights agenda was also marginalised. Through the Afghan Women's Network, consultations with women were conducted nationwide on the matter of conceptualizing the framework for sustainable peace. However, their recommendations were not incorporated into the final strategy for Afghanistan's security transition beyond 2014.

Given the continuing marginalisation of our agenda, where do women stand in the pursuit of sustainable peace? Our first major concern is the return of Talibanism. To us, Talibanism is a terrorist ideology perpetrated by violence and sustained by the oppression of women. The reason that the Taliban is so adamant in its oppression of women is because women's oppression is the only key to intergenerational perpetuation of Taliban control. Oppressing half of the population is winning half of the war. Depriving women of education spawns generations of ignorant people who will submit to subjugation with uncomplaining docility. The use of domestic violence in order to control women and girls embeds in children at a very young age the ideology that sustains Talibanism. When women are scared, fear is handed down in magnified proportions from generation to generation. When women have no voice, society learns that voicelessness is the norm. The international community must recognize that the main issue is not simply a denial of women's rights; rather, the perpetuation of Talibanism through the oppression of women's rights is a core issue in our transition to sustainable peace.

This core issue brings with it a number of related concerns, one of which is the exclusion of women from the peace process. Our government has been systematically marginalizing women in consultations and decisionmaking processes because of its shallow understanding of the dynamics between women's oppression and Talibanism. Like the Taliban, the government does not respect the views of women, and they do not wish to recognize that women have perspectives that could enrich decision making. In this particular case, the exclusion of women is not only a denial of women's rights. More than anything, it is a rejection of the opportunity to benefit from perspectives that could substantially strengthen Afghanistan's strategy for dealing with the Taliban.

Another related issue is the strong possibility that women's rights will be discarded in the name of peace. Unfortunately for women what the Taliban value as a top bargaining chip appears trivial to our leaders. President Karzai demonstrated his indifference when he supported a recent declaration of our religious council, which, among other provisions, directs society to adhere to a doctrine of women's subjugation and gives men the power to control women.

And how do Afghans protect the international community's investments and the reconstruction process of the past decade? Despite enormous setbacks, Afghans have made modest gains and are now optimistic about the future. Afghan women have been granted equality in relation to men, at least in the law and through certain policies. Our girls and young women are back in schools; our professional women are, for the most part, employed; Afghan women can travel abroad and secure protection and services when they need them; they can participate in elections and public life; and they can dream of a better life. Afghan women are happy that there are episodes of peace, even if they are continuously disrupted. Afghans are grateful that the international community has helped them restore democracy and human rights, even if they are not fully enjoyed by many. Afghan women can live because they have hope. All these experiences and realities deepen our fear of a potential Taliban resurgence. Life continues to be enormously difficult for many Afghans, but it is a life far sweeter than one lived under Taliban rule.

Recommendations

When you are abused, attacked, beaten, and veiled
when you are tortured, strangled, choked and slaved
you feel numbness, nothingness, lifeless with tears
you are a shadow, a ghost a creature with many fears

I feel that it is important that my book on Afghan women also include recommendations to my audience. By all indications, the gains that Afghan women have made during the past decade are bound to be lost once our rights are traded off in the peace process. These recommendations were prepared to reflect the perspectives and concerns of women in communities that are hardly reached by development and are often missed by national reconstruction initiatives. The analysis, comments, and recommendations raised in this book are crucial in helping reverse the rapid downward spiral of women's rights in this critical phase of security and political transition in our country. In order to prevent our rights from disappearing, Afghani women require your help in the following ways:

1. Help us get our leaders genuinely committed to women's rights as they commit to the peace process. Your senior

diplomats and officials could help by communicating our issues to Afghanistan's leaders. There are several ways to do this: (a) send a joint communiqué (to be signed by various diplomatic missions to Afghanistan) to our president containing a ten-point women's agenda in the peace process; (b) organize a delegation (of the signatories to the communiqué) to meet with the president and senior peace officials for the purpose of adopting the recommendations; and (c) support a high-level technical meeting to work out the details of the agenda's implementation, funding, and monitoring.

2. Assist us in establishing an independent body (unlike the Ministry of Women's Affairs, which is subject to the authority of the President) to act as an oversight committee and to hold our senior officials accountable for women's issues in the peace process. If this is not possible, help us request the United Nations Commission on the Status of Women to form a special task force within the Committee on the Elimination of All Forms of Discrimination against Women to monitor and hear complaints on women's issues in the pursuit of sustainable peace in Afghanistan.
3. Evaluate the achievements of the peace process at least every two years, including its achievements in building upon the gains of the past decade, particularly gains on the protection, promotion, and fulfillment of women's rights.
4. Help us to remove from power leaders who cannot serve as custodians of the people's trust. In the coming election, the international media should expose the track records of candidates and prevent the international community from providing logistical support to those who have records of human rights violations. More importantly, consider how the politics of peace will change under the leadership of nontraditional politicians. Think about supporting female presidential candidates; and help us get a woman appointed as the next vice president.
5. Invest in ongoing capacity building and the sensitisation of law enforcement and security institutions to women's rights

in the context of sustainable peace. Educate high-ranking officials on the strategic value of women's empowerment for the eradication of Talibanism in the country. Help us develop the tools needed to promote women's empowerment as a tactical weapon against flourishing Taliban ideology.

6. Oppose any effort to amend the existing constitutional provisions, laws, and policies on gender equality. Withdraw support from projects that do not show clear contributions to women's empowerment. Call for the imposition of an indefinite moratorium on the adoption of new laws and policies that will alter substantive gender equality, especially in the name of peace and religion.
7. Fund the development of a women's human rights watch report that could be published annually in order to provide evidence-based information on the impact of the security transition and sustainable peace on women. Assist in the dissemination of such information globally and help draw attention to the issues captured by the report.
8. Help educate the average Afghan woman of how the Afghan law, international human rights law, and even Islam safeguard women's right and gender equality.
9. Create a quota to ensure the participation of women in various government departments.
10. The current gender strategies and plans for the development and growth of women in Afghanistan need to be monitored and implemented with full faith. Basic literacy training should be provided to both men and women to reduce incidents of domestic violence.
11. Security forces, administrative officials, the police force, and the judiciary should be trained and educated on human rights connected to women and gender related issues.
12. Create employment opportunities for women through a host of vocational training programs or micro credit schemes to enable women to generate income.
13. Special training should be targeted at providing support and service to widowed, divorced, or otherwise single women;

with special focus on protecting them from sexual violence and exploitation.

14. Awareness must be created about the considerable number of women who are perpetrators of domestic violence directly or indirectly and that such acts are a crime under both the law and religion.
15. The government needs to ensure that efforts to address issues like domestic violence and forced marriage are not limited to urban areas but are implemented in rural regions and the far-flung areas of the south eastern border zone, where such cases are more likely to take place.
16. Make it more feasible for women to talk about domestic violence in order to bring them out of the belief that they are isolated in their experience. Emphasize Article 44 of the Afghan Constitution that protects the right to education. Public services need to send out strong messages that communicate that any kind of violence against women is a crime.
17. Educate the masses about the relation between domestic violence and the lack of a woman's knowledge of her husband before marriage to encourage families to allow their daughters to get better acquainted with their husbands before marriage, even though the marriage is arranged by the family.
18. Help ensure an ending to child marriage, forced marriage, polygamy, and other such traditional and cultural practices that worsen the plight of women. Involve more and more women and ensure their participation in designing, planning, and implementing measures that will bring positive changes into the lives of women.
19. The government needs to increase the number of clinics that provide health services to mothers and children in villages and should provide midwifery trainings so as to lower women's death rate during pregnancy or child birth. More female health professionals are needed.
20. The government needs to provide security to female lawyers, judges, and prosecutors. The number of women in the Afghan

police force needs to be increased significantly since women police officers better understand the situations related to women and can handle them with the delicacy that is required. Women entrepreneurs should be encouraged and provided long-term loans.

We have consulted widely to arrive at the position listed above, and we have made further recommendations in the report prepared by the Afghan Women's Network and the Jalal Foundation, which is accessible on the Jalal Foundation website. Those recommendations include:

1. The implementation of the government's strategy should be thoroughly evaluated before 2014. Unless it is able to show compelling success, the strategy should be aborted or amended as appropriate;
2. The international community should help Afghans get rid of incompetent leaders. Our leaders of today do not value women's empowerment because they themselves were raised in homes embedded in women's oppression. They do not see the strategic and political reasons behind the Taliban's obsession to oppress Afghan women. In the forthcoming election, the international media should expose the track records of the candidates and push harder for the election of more qualified women. Help women NGOs to work for a "women's vote" that will transform election politics and the quality of leaders in our country;
3. Security and law enforcement officers must be sensitized to the strategic and political reasons behind the Taliban's obsessive interest in women's oppression. At the moment, police and military training focuses on the importance of respecting women's rights. Although this emphasis is important, the training should put even greater emphasis on analyzing the Taliban agenda to attain continuous, intergenerational control by oppressing women's rights. Trainees need to see that women's empowerment is a potent antidote to Talibanism and find ways to optimize this advantage;

4. Help us establish an independent high level mechanism that has the authority, resources, and capacity to resolve the violation of women's rights. Before the end of the term of the current president, the Commission on the Status of Women should ask him to report on the performance of his administration in regard to women's rights; and
5. Oppose any effort to amend the constitutional and other legal instruments on gender equality. Call for the imposition of an indefinite moratorium to the adoption of new laws and policies that will alter substantive gender equality, especially in the name of peace and religion.

Notes

1. Statistics from this section were taken from the report on Afghanistan by the UN Secretary General to the UN General Assembly for the period January to March 2012.

Conclusion

English novelist Clive Staples Lewis once said that pain is a scream from God. He said that "God whispers to us in our pleasures, speaks to us in our conscience, but shouts to us in our pains. It is his megaphone to rouse a deaf world." Afghan women live in a political climate where aspirations to democracy easily turn into tragedy. Nowadays, the rule of law exists only for the powerless, and those who have guns prevail through tyranny and despotism, as it was during the Taliban regime. Have Afghan women been abandoned by the international community of democratic nations? How could they introduce the concept of democracy in this country and then leave us to fight an unfinished battle against its enemies, alone?

The increase in violence directed at females—such as the poisoning of girls, the execution and assassination of women, and the victimisation of women through domestic violence throughout the country—begs for the creation of a national mechanism to oversee the expeditious resolution of such cases. Afghan women call upon our government to either expand the mandate of the Commission on Violence Against Women to include a quick, dedicated response to VAW cases or to create a supplementary mechanism that will work not only on policy recommendations but also on case resolution. Afghan women also call for increased resources and training for community police in order to strengthen their capacity to combat crimes, particularly those directed towards women.

The ongoing violence confirms the magnitude of the challenge of protecting women and their defenders, and securing their rights by the end of 2014. On behalf of Afghan women, I call upon human rights groups and women's organisations to look beyond traditional solutions and to be our megaphone. Afghan women simply cannot afford to do nothing while the killings of our sisters continue. Violence against women is a matter of concern to all Afghans, women and men alike. Today, it is "they;" tomorrow, it could be your mother, sister, daughter, or yourself.

I encourage you to look at the Jalal Foundation and the Afghan Women's Network in order to view the many recommendations engendered by nationwide consultation with Afghan women. As a marginalised group, we count on new, progressive leaders who are open to alternative perspectives that never find a way into strategic decision making. We need to be in this together. Leaders promote enduring peace and democracy by counting women in; stop viewing women's rights as an issue that merely complicates the problem of, and solution to, peace and security; see women's rights as an antidote to long-term Talibanism. Armed with this approach, enduring peace can be attained.

Part–II

Afghan's Rights and Security Transition Post 2014

Dr Mario Silva

Introduction

Since the September 11, 2001, terrorist attacks on New York and Washington, the topics of state failure, terrorism, humanitarian intervention, and postconflict reconstruction have ranked high on the US and international community agenda. With the upcoming transition of power following the presidential elections in 2014, the international community's concern about terrorism and instability is increasing, especially in the lawless mountainous region of Afghanistan-Pakistan. Whereas the Taliban-linked Al Qaeda regime was ousted from power following Operation Enduring Freedom in 2001, the terrorist group and its affiliates continue to thrive not just along the border but also in several parts of the Middle East and Africa.

Afghanistan's neighbours are understandably nervous about what will happen to security and stability in the region after the International Security Assistance Force leaves Afghanistan in December 2014. The situation in neighbouring Pakistan is even more problematic with state instability, sectarian strife, and Taliban insurgents operating along border regions.

State failure in Afghanistan has created several humanitarian, security, and legal challenges for the international community. During the Taliban, violence and criminal economic activity thrived, and terrorists benefited from the prevailing anarchy. The question of whether the international community responded effectively in order to deal with state failure and whether NATO and its allies provided the Afghan National Security Forces with the necessary tools to prevent future ongoing security threats is still to be answered. The conflict in Afghanistan is one of the longest contemporary conflicts, and a huge investment with heavy loss of life has been made to keep the peace and force the terrorists from power; however, reconstruction of a failed state like Afghanistan entails long-term investments and commitments by member states and willing partners.

After decades of civil war, which left widespread human suffering, and with the ouster of the Taliban, many euphorically hoped that the people of Afghanistan would attain full and equal rights. Progress was made— particularly in education, health, and gender equality—with many women working hard to reverse the damage brought by internal conflict and war. However, while many positive steps have been taken forward in reconstruction, Afghan people continue to suffer from deteriorating security, political struggles between warring factions, and a thriving narcotics trade. Women have been left out of the peace process. Corruption is rampant, with the president even admitting that he receives bags of cash from the Iranian government. Afghanistan is ranked 175th of 177 countries on Transparency International's Corruption Perception Index.[1]

With presidential elections and a new incoming administration, the opportunity for change remains; but with it, a danger that many hard-won political, economic, and social gains since the overthrow of the Taliban may be rolled back (see Part I). The hope of the international community is that Afghanistan maintains long-term security and stability with respect for the rule of law and does not revert to a collapsed state following the scheduled exit in 2014. Afghans' rights and security are once again at a crossroad.

Notes

1. "Afghanistan is advancing towards stability as international force draws down – UN envoy," UN News, 17 December 2013. Available at: http://www.un.org/apps/news/ story.asp?NewsID=46762#.Us3me_RDuSo

Chapter 1

Summary of Operations

Pre-9/11 Afghanistan

Once known to be a land of fearless tribal chiefs and free-spirited people, Afghanistan today is but a miserable reflection of its ancient glory. In the past three decades, it has been a victim of chronic wars, murder, mayhem, conflict, and instability. Afghanistan's ancient and proud people are today scattered all over the world as refugees.

This landlocked territory has continuously been fought over. It lies sandwiched between Central Asia, India, and the Middle East. As part of the Silk Route, it was always valuable, in spite of its rather forbidding and rugged terrain.[1] Afghanistan shares its border with Iran in the west, Pakistan in the south, Uzbekistan, Turkmenistan, and Tajikistan in the north, and China in the far northeast.[2]

The territory that is now defined as Afghanistan emerged in the late eighteenth century and was ruled by a succession of monarchs. The borders were delineated as a result of "The Great Game" between Britain and Russia in the late nineteenth century. Britain continued to exert influence until the Third Anglo-Afghan War in 1919. With the creation of the League of Nations in 1919, a result of the Paris Peace Conference, the existence of Afghanistan as a matter of law has remained effectively unchallenged.

In 1973, Muhammad Daud overthrew his cousin King Zahir Shah and declared a republic. The Cold War was on, and both the United States and the Soviet Union were keen to get a grip in the region.

However, in 1978, Daud was killed in a communist coup led by the Afghanistan's People's Democratic Party. The Soviet Union took advantage of the resultant political unrest and chaos, and President Brezhnev sent in troops in December 1979.

The Security Council considered a response to the invasion but a draft resolution condemning it was not passed due to the Soviet Union's veto powers. However, the General Assembly held an emergency special session on Afghanistan in January 1980 and adopted Resolution ES-6/2, deploring the armed intervention and calling for the withdrawal of all foreign forces.[3]

The Soviet Union installed the puppet government of Babrak Kamal,[4] while the neighboring country of Pakistan began recruiting Mujahideen fighters to wage a holy war against the Soviets. Pakistan was given financial support by Saudi Arabia and the United States, with reported estimates that between 1986 to 1990, weapons worth US$5 billion were sent to the Mujahideen.[5] It is estimated that one hundred thousand Pakistanis fought and trained with the Taliban from 1994 to 2001, with Saudi Arabia providing the necessary funds to support the regime. Among the supporters was the now notorious, wealthy Saudi terrorist named Osama bin Laden.[6]

In 1989, the new Russian president, Mikhail Gorbachev, withdrew the USSR forces, leaving an estimated 1.5 million Afghans dead, five million disabled, an equal number of Afghan refugees, and fourteen thousand Soviet soldiers dead.[7] The coming years would lead to further killings and displacements of people.

In April 1992, the Mujahideen took Kabul and claimed an Islamic state. There was serious discord, however, between the various commanders, and with the help of Pakistan, a new group launched a military campaign with the objective of creating an Islamic state based on Sharia law. On September 27, 1996, the Islamic Emirate of Afghanistan was established. The Taliban version of Islam and Sharia was extreme, harsh, and dogmatic. Intellectuals and women were the worst affected, and human rights violations such as torture, killings, and rapes intensified.

The government was promptly recognised by Pakistan, Saudi Arabia, and United Arab Emirates. Relations with the United States were tenuous due to the Taliban sheltering Osama bin Laden, whom the United States suspected of masterminding the US embassy attacks in Nairobi and Dar-es-Salam. In October 1996, the UN Security Council imposed Resolution 1076[8] to halt the hostilities and terrorism activities. Following the August 7, 1998, terrorist bomb attacks on US embassies in Nairobi, Kenya, and Dar-es-Salaam, Tanzania, the Security Council adopted Resolution 1193,[9] which repeated the concern at the continuing presence of terrorists in the territory of Afghanistan.[10]

The Taliban seized power during the vacuum that was left after the Soviet Union withdrew from Afghanistan and adopted an extreme interpretation of Islamic law, waging a vicious war against women. Several international reports noted the hapless condition of women in Afghanistan. Under the totalitarian dictatorship established by the Taliban, women and girls were denied the most fundamental human rights. They were given only the most basic access to health care (they were banned from being treated by male doctors), and girls were denied an education. The burqa became mandatory. Women could not attend university, play sports, or laugh in public. Not a single area of a woman's daily life remained unregulated. Those women who could not afford a burqa or did not have a male relative to accompany them could never leave their houses. With the strict application of Sharia law, movies, songs, dancing, and even clapping were forbidden, and many women were whipped and some even stoned to death.

Human rights violations continued unabated, with the international community unwilling to act to stop the Al Qaeda terrorist network of Osama bin Laden, the increasing oppression of women, the destruction of Afghanistan's cultural heritage, and the production of illicit opium[11]—until the 2001 attacks on US soil.

Post-9/11: Legitimate Use of Force

Following the murder of three thousand people on the soil of the United States on September 11, 2001, by the Afghan-based Al Qaeda group, on November 14, the Security Council unanimously adopted Resolution 1378 and called for the establishment of a transitional administration leading to the formation of a new government. The Security Council was concerned with the continuing serious violations of human rights and international humanitarian law. Acting under Chapter VII of the UN Charter, the Council provided support for international efforts to root out terrorism and recognised the

> urgency of the security and political situation in Afghanistan in light of the most recent developments, particularly in Kabul...for allowing Afghanistan to be used as a base for the export of terrorism by the Al-Qaida network and other terrorist groups and for providing safe haven to Usama Bin Laden, Al-Qaida and others associated with them, and in this context supporting the efforts of the Afghan people to replace the Taliban regime.[12]

Most legal experts would argue that the humanitarian interventions in Afghanistan following September 11, 2011, provided much needed legitimacy to military actions that were undertaken by the United States and NATO. However, it is worth noting that the international community generally acknowledged Operation Enduring Freedom as justified because its intentions ranged from humanitarian intervention to self-defense. The war on terrorism, however, was much broader in scope and included issues concerning preemptive war, the legitimacy of humanitarian intervention, and self-defense that threatens international peace and security—issues that continue to be controversial in international law.

The international community's response following the terrorist attacks in New York and Washington emphasized security and humanitarian concerns but also collective self-defense and the war on terror. The military engagement in Iraq in 2003, officially based on humanitarian grounds, was more problematic than that of Afghanistan in 2001. Some argued that the Iraq military intervention diverted attention from the hiding of Al Qaeda fighters in Pakistan and the terrorist activity that was taking place in Afghanistan; further, the engagement in Iraq weakened the argument for humanitarian intervention in the future.

The terrorist attacks in New York and Washington led the Bush administration to describe terrorism as the greatest threat to peace and to officially launch the formation of the American National Security Strategy in September 2002. Its strategic goals included "political and economic freedom, peaceful relations with other states, and respect for human dignity."[13] And in order to achieve these objectives, the United States promised to "champion aspirations for human dignity; strengthen alliances to defeat global terrorism and work to prevent attacks against us and our friends."[14]

The National Security Strategy's purpose was based on the view that the "United States of America is fighting a war against terrorists of global reach. The enemy is not a single political regime or person or religion or ideology. The enemy is terrorism—premeditated, politically motivated violence perpetrated against innocents."[15]

The threat of terrorism led the United States to adopt the doctrine of preemptive self-defense, which raised the issue of the legitimate use of force in international law; in the case of Afghanistan, the United States and its allies did adhere to, and acted as mandated by, the UN Charter.

The UN Security Council also declared terrorism a "threat to international peace and security," as noted in Resolution 1368. This declaration has lead to an increased focus by most world governments on national security and the precautions necessary to be taken against the transnational threat of terrorism.

On September 14, 2001, Congress passed legislation authorizing the use of force, which President Bush signed into law on September 18, 2001. Use of Military Force Against Terrorists authorised the US Armed Forces to use force against those responsible for the attacks. The White House declared the Taliban "terrorists" rather than "soldiers" and did not seek a declaration of war by Congress, therefore deeming the operation to be outside the protection of the Geneva Convention. This position led to several legal challenges and was eventually overruled by the US Supreme Court in 2008.

The invasion of Afghanistan was a legitimate act of self-defense by the United Nations after the 9/11 attacks. First, the concept of self-defense is recognised by the Charter of the United Nations, Article 51:

> Nothing in the present Charter shall impair the inherent right of individual or collective self-defence if an armed attack occurs

> against a Member of the United Nations... until the Security Council has taken measures necessary to maintain international peace and security. Measures taken by Members in the exercise of this right of self-defence shall be immediately reported to the Security Council and shall not in any way affect the authority and responsibility of the Security Council under the present Charter to take at any time such action as it deems necessary in order to maintain or restore international peace and security.[16]

Afghanistan was an aggressor state since the attacks were perpetrated by agents who were working with the Taliban regime, and there was justified concern that following 9/11, Afghanistan, which harbored terrorists, could launch another attack on the United States and other Western nations. The threat of new attacks was deemed imminent. Furthermore, Osama Bin Laden, a power broker in Afghan politics, acknowledged Al Qaeda's authorship of the attacks.

The primary goal of the US and NATO engagement in Afghanistan was to overthrow the Taliban regime and to destroy Al Qaeda; but also claiming a prominent position was the liberation of the Afghan people—especially girls and women—from the brutal oppressive regime of the Taliban. The war on the Taliban by the United States and its allies was thus justified as an exercise in self-defense and an operation to prevent further crimes against humanity and to punish perpetrators of such crimes. Humanitarian concerns, including mass violations of human rights, were regarded as posing a "threat to international peace and security," and action was taken according to Chapter VII of the UN Charter.

Thus, the war in Afghanistan was directed by the United Nations with full international legal authority under Chapter VII of the UN Charter. In addition, for the first time, NATO invoked Article V of the North Atlantic Treaty on October 4, 2001, which provides that an armed attack against any NATO country is considered an attack against the Alliance.

Between September 11 and October 7, 2001, when the bombardment of Afghanistan began, the UN Security Council adopted Resolution 1368 of September 12, which stated that the Council "unequivocally condemns in the strongest terms the horrifying terrorist attacks ...and regards such acts, like any act of international terrorism, as a threat to international peace and security." In addition, Resolution 1378 of November 14, 2001, condemns the Taliban and supports "the efforts of the Afghan people to replace the Taliban regime." Likewise, Security Council Resolution 1383 of December 6, 2001, ratifies the Bonn Agreement signed the day before, providing for temporary arrangements among the "coalition" countries and the representatives of their Afghan allies in the formation of a new administration in Afghanistan.

The words "enduring freedom" appeared in Resolution 1510 of October 13, 2003, and authorised the expansion of the International Security Assistance Force. The international community, through the United Nations, also has the responsibility to use appropriate diplomatic, humanitarian, and other means, in accordance with Chapters VI and VIII of the Charter, to help protect populations from inter alia genocide, war crimes, ethnic cleansing, and crimes against humanity. In this context, the Security Council was prepared to take collective action in accordance with the Charter, including Chapter VII. The Security Council has the full authority and legitimacy under international law to deem what events constitute a threat to peace and security.

Shortly following the attacks, the US Government sought United Nations backing for military action, and as noted in Security Council Resolution 1368 of September 12, 2001, the Council, "expresses its readiness to take all necessary steps to respond [implying force] to the September 11 attacks." Some critics note that the resolution authorised neither military action in response to the attacks nor Operation Enduring Freedom to oust the Taliban. However, the implications for the members of the Security Council were far reaching. They were fully aware of the consequences of putting in a motion authorizing all necessary measures and stating the need for a response to threats to international peace and security.

The US Congress passed a resolution that was signed by President Bush on September 18, 2011, which was more explicit than the UN Resolution, authorizing "all necessary and appropriate force against those nations, organisations, or persons he determines planned, authorised, committed, or aided the terrorist attacks that occurred on September 11, 2001, *or harbored such organisations or persons*."[17]

The terrorist attacks on September 11, 2001, shifted America and the international community of nations towards the realisation that what takes places in one region can have consequences in another. The attitude towards humanitarian intervention became more favorable. However, emphasis has remained on the concern for domestic security. Analyses of humanitarian interventions have shown inconsistencies; for example, the appalling situation in Darfur, which some have called genocide, garnered little attention following 9/11. Darfur did not fit the war on terrorism's security and strategic interests. Even following the adoption of the responsibility to protect doctrine, Darfur still failed to draw the necessary attention.

The 2002 National Security Strategy proposed a new policy of preemptive action against terrorists. The new action plan for the defense of the United States and its interests at home and abroad included "identifying and destroying the threat before it reaches our borders,"[18] and although the United States would endeavor to enlist the support of the international community, the States would "not hesitate to act alone, if necessary, to exercise our rights of self-defense by acting preemptively against such terrorists, to prevent them from doing harm against our people and our country."[19] This new doctrine—of having the right to attack unilaterally to prevent a perceived serious threat to a country's vital interests or those of its allies—came to challenge the international community following the invasion of Iraq. The wars in Afghanistan and in Iraq were waged as part of the Bush administration's war on terrorism and liberation of people from oppressive regimes. However, the March 2003 invasion of Iraq without UN Security Council approval weakened and diverted much-needed attention in Afghanistan, which allowed for the insurgency to grow.

Operation Enduring Freedom

Operation Enduring Freedom was the official name the United States gave to the military operation in Afghanistan. It began on October 7, 2001, and consisted initially of US and UK air strikes on Taliban and Al Qaeda forces, with the purpose of ousting the Taliban and assisting the Northern Alliance-[20] forces. In early November, countries such as Australia, Canada, France, Germany, The Netherlands, Poland, and Turkey announced their intention to deploy troops to Afghanistan. A month after Operation Enduring Freedom was launched, the Taliban quickly lost support, and the regime unraveled after losing its stronghold city of Mazar-e-Sharif on November 9, 2001.

The Northern Alliance initially assembled key Tajik leaders and, in 2000, anti-Taliban Pashtun forces to fight a defensive war against the Taliban, which was heavily supported by Pakistan. On December 7, 2001, Afghan opposition forces, led by General Abdul Rashid Dostum of the Northern Alliance force, took control of Kandahar.[21] The defunct Taliban regime, led by their spiritual leader and Head of the Supreme Council Mullah Mohammad Omar,[22] quickly fled Kandahar with most of the Taliban leadership and its Al Qaeda allies, and headed for Pakistan.

Following Operation Enduring Freedom's remarkable combat success, the international community mobilised to create a transition administration in post-Taliban Afghanistan. Continuing to promote dialogue among the various Taliban resistance parties, the United Nations organised a meeting of Afghan political leaders in Bonn, Germany, in late November 2001. The Bonn Conference resulted in the creation of the Afghan Interim Authority. On December 22, Hamid Karzai, a Pashtun leader, was sworn in as the head of the interim, power-sharing government.[23]

International Security Assistance Force

An emergency meeting of the *loya jirga*[24] established the Afghan Transitional Authority in June 2002. Karzai was elected president of the Islamic Republic of Afghanistan in 2004.

In December 2001, the Security Council established the International Security Assistance Force to oversee security in the country and to train the Afghan National Security Forces. The initial authorisation was based on Resolution 1386, for a period of six months. The Security Council gave the International Security Assistance Force the mandate "to continue to work in close consultation with the Afghan

Transitional Authority and its successors and the Special Representative of the Secretary General as well as with the Operation Enduring Freedom."[25]

The mandate has been extended regularly, and the agreement also provided for progressive expansion of the International Security Assistance Force. Acting under Chapter VII of the Charter and having determined that the situation in Afghanistan still constituted a threat to international peace and security,[26] the Security Council unanimously adopted Resolution 1510 (2003), and the force was expanded to other urban centers beyond Kabul.

In August 2003, NATO assumed leadership of the International Security Forces Administration and provided the core force with assistance from troops from forty-three countries. With the resurgence of Taliban fighters, Afghanistan remains a difficult and challenging operation for NATO and its partners. The security situation is still weak, and whether the Afghan army will have the capacity to take on the insurgents and provide security for this failed state post 2014 is doubtful.

Notes

1. During the Pre-Islamic period, there are many stories from that of Alexander the Great (356-323 BC) to that of Darius the Great of Persia and other civilisations until in 699 AD an Arab raid on Kandahar ushered in Islam in the region.
2. Afghan Profile, BBC News, 24 November 2013. Available at: http:// www.bbc.co.uk/ news/world-south-asia-12011352.
3. Afghan & the United Nations, UN News, 24 January 2014.
4. Afghan in Brief, Embassy of Afghanistan, Washington DC, 24 January 2014.
5. Kenneth Katzman, Afghanistan: Post-Taliban Governance, Security, and U.S. Policy, Congressional Research Service, 23 October 2013.
6. For more information see article by Eric Lichtblau and Eric Schmitt, "Cash Flow to Terrorists Evades U.S. Efforts," New York Times, 5 December 2010.
7. Afghan & the United Nations, UN News, 24 January 2014.
8. *Ibid.*
9. "Security Council Strongly Condemns Terrorist Bomb Attacks in Nairobi and Dar Es Salaam on 7 August," UN News, 13 August 1998.

10. Afghan & the United Nations, UN News, 24 January 2014.
11. *Ibid.*
12. Security Council Sets United Nations Course for Supporting New Governance in Afghanistan; Urges No Reprisals , Resolution 1378, Adopted Unanimously, Anticipates Broad-Based, Multi-Ethnic Transitional Administration, Leading to New Government, 14 November 2001. At: http:/ /www.un.org/News/Press/docs/2001/sc7212. doc.htm
13. The National Security Strategy of the United States of America, September 2002. Available at: http://www.state.gov/documents/organisation/63562.pdf
14. *Ibid.*
15. *Ibid.*
16. UN Charter was signed on 26 June 1945, by 50 of the 51 original member countries and entered into force on 24 October 1945 (Poland, the other original member, which was not represented at the conference, signed it two months later).
17. The National Defense Authorisation Act (NDAA) is a piece of United States legislation passed every year to authorize the defense budget. More at: http://ndaa2012. us/#sthash.IhqMvhSN.dpuf
18. The National Security Strategy of the United States of America, September 2002. Available at: http://www.state.gov/documents/organisation/63562.pdf
19. *Ibid.*
20. The Northern Alliance, officially known as the United Islamic Front for the Salvation of Afghanistan came to formation after the Taliban regime came to power and established the Islamic Emirate of Afghanistan in 1996.
21. General Dostum is considered to be the leader of the Uzbek community and is part of the leadership council of the National Front of Afghanistan.
22. Omar (Umar) was Afghanistan's de facto 11th head of state from 1996 to late 2001, under the official title "Head of the Supreme Council". He held the title Commander of the Faithful of the Islamic Emirate of Afghanistan, which was recognised by only three nations: Pakistan, Saudi Arabia, and the United Arab Emirates. For further information see: http://www.princeton.edu/~achaney/tmve/wiki100k/docs/Mohammed_Omar.html
23. More information available at: http://www.cnn.com/2013/10/28/world/ operationenduring- freedom-fast-facts/
24. Pashto for grand council—a traditional forum of tribal elders.
25. Security Council Seeks Expansion of Role of International Efforts in Afghanistan, to Extend Beyond Kabul, Resolution 1510 (2003). Adopted Unanimously, Urges Measures to Fulfil Mandate of Force; Situation Said to Remain Threat to Peace and Security, 13 October 2003. Avalable at: http://www.un.org/News/Press/docs/2003/ sc7894.doc.htm
26. *Ibid.*

Chapter 2

State Failure and Reconstruction

State Failure

Failed states result from a temporary or prolonged loss of appropriate institutions, which create a structural competency deficit. Structural competency includes the provision of security and basic political goods. State failure[1] has significant consequences for the international community, eventually requiring its intervention in order to bring about stability. State failure in Afghanistan has been characterised by an implosion of structural competency as well as instability, which creates a vacuum that various groups, including armed factions and terrorists, readily occupy. A flow of refugees has resulted in instability extending to neighbouring states. The accumulation of structural competency deficits owing to inappropriate institutions, which evolve over a period of time, results in state failure. Long before the September 11 attacks, the United Nations had the legal authority and should have acted to prevent the collapse of international human rights and humanitarian law.

Throughout the 1990s, the concept of failed states was increasingly linked to international insecurity and nontraditional security threats. Helman and Ratner brought attention to this phenomenon and sought to point out the security implications of failed states. After the attacks on September 11, 2011, "failed state" became the prevailing term that was used in national security circles to describe the phenomenon. The events of 9/11 created a sense of urgency with respect to addressing the challenges of state failure and to the threats that failed states pose to international security.

In Afghanistan, human security even after the Soviet occupation was constantly threatened by widespread violence, internal conflict, and terrorism. These conditions inevitably lead to a loss of territorial control and to political instability. According to Stephen Walt of Harvard University, when "governments collapse, the resulting anarchy often triggers largescale migration, economic chaos, and mass violence."[2] State failure in Afghanistan not only constitutes an undeniable threat to the lives of the people living there but also poses a considerable threat to world peace, as has been demonstrated by the conflicts that followed 9/11.

In Afghanistan, for example, Al Qaeda took advantage of a weak government, finding sanctuary in ungoverned territory; the "lack of institutional mechanisms to deal with crises suggests that the costs of terrorism are greater in fragile states—a conclusion too obvious to debate."[3] The lack of internal security provides an explanation of how Afghanistan became a failed state.

Reconstruction efforts by the international community have met with mixed success. Women's (and girls') equal rights, as outlined in the Afghan Constitution, have not been protected, and this state of affairs has been viewed critically. The reconstruction of the rule of law, security, and development have been complicated by the various terrorist activities that are still taking place.[4] Transnational terrorist organisations, such as Al Qaeda, have benefited from Afghanistan's state failure since it provides them with a safe haven, enabling them to recruit members and build training camps.

State failure presents a multitude of challenges for the international community. Given the complex nature and instabilities of a failed state, it may arguably have been in the best interests of the Afghan people for the international community to have retained an active role. Sharing sovereignty in some capacity to address the many issues affecting Afghanistan's structural competency, which caused it to fail in the first place, may well have been a favorable option.

Failed states rarely exist in isolation and have often been referred to as Petri dishes[5] for transnational criminal activity, arms smuggling, human trafficking, and terrorism and as sources of drug production. In the post-9/11 era, terrorism has come to be regarded as acts of aggression analogous to an interstate armed conflict, and therefore the term "war on terror" has emerged.

Events in Afghanistan remind us of the cruelty and suffering that is endured by those who live in a failed state. In today's increasingly interconnected world, a failed state represents a regional and potentially global threat. Efforts to promote sustainable peace and stability will inevitably entail not just peacekeeping measures but also the means to influence the choices that failed states make regarding their development.

At the time of the military intervention in Afghanistan by the international community, Secretary-General Kofi Annan described the failed states reconstruction situation as immense:

> They include the reintegration of former combatants; revival of economic activity; a fairer justice system, democratic institutions and mechanisms to protect human rights; such basic serves as clean water, sanitation, schools, health care and roads; ensuring the country is no longer a haven for terrorists or drug traffickers; ending violence against women; protecting children's' rights; and ensuring security throughout the country.[6]

It was for that reason that many donor countries met at the Tokyo Conference and pledged over $4.5 billion for reconstruction.

Much has changed since the days of the Westphalian concept of statehood. The current era is one of globalisation, which has led to a debate over the implications of state sovereignty and the Westphalian system. Today, there is a fully interconnected global order where what happens in one state has an impact on another. With the emergence of regional and international law—especially human rights law—the notion of state sovereignty has been challenged. States have a responsibility to protect their citizens and ensure that human rights law is adhered to. Various international law treaties chart the important responsibilities that states have in respecting international law conventions and in providing security for their constituents.

European states found themselves in Afghanistan, in the first place, from a sense of solidarity following the 9/11 attacks and the 2004 and 2005 bombings in Madrid and London, and in the second place, owing to a broader humanitarian concern regarding human rights and the need to stabilize failed states.[7]

Postconflict Reconstruction

The United Nations has played a leadership role in the political process in Afghanistan as well as managing humanitarian assistance. Providing security and establishing respect for rule of law are crucial elements of the postconflict reconstruction in Afghanistan. During reconstruction efforts in failed states, the cooperation of different political factions is needed to promote stability and peace, as most of these states are prone to having power consolidated in the hands of a few individuals or groups. It has also been seen that some of these groups have a stake in the conflict because war has often allowed them to profit either economically or politically. The pursuit of state reconstruction and the avoidance of state failure caused by civil war drives home the importance of governance in establishing peace, which helps avoid conflict in the first place. The need to construct new institutions and reconstruct weakened or collapsed ones is critical in failed states, and the challenges are particularly pressing.

Legitimacy is extremely important, the loss of legitimacy being a key factor in state failure. Reconstituting legitimacy should involve expanding the participation of various groups, reestablishing rule of law, and holding free and fair elections. In almost all cases of state failure, political reconstruction and renewal have involved elections. These postconflict elections carry a tremendous burden, as they are organised under difficult circumstances with minimal security. Elections serve as important opportunities for rebuilding institutions and transitioning to democracy—long-term processes that are not simply about one particular election. What needs to be built is a "political system that encourages government, political, business and civic leaders to articulate and pursue objectives that are centered around people and a system that promotes public consensus on these objectives."[8] In order to establish national consensus, objectives that have legitimacy in the eyes of the people are required.

Reconstituting legitimacy entails "expanding participation and inclusiveness, reducing inequities, creating accountability, combating corruption and introducing contestability (elections)."[9] According to the 2001 UN Development Program report, democracy is the governing system with the strongest legitimacy:

> Democracy has proven to be the system of governance most capable of mediating and preventing conflict and of securing and sustaining wellbeing. By expanding people's choices about how and by whom they are governed, democracy brings principles of participation and accountability to the process of human development.[10]

The report further argues that for "politics and political institutions to promote human development and safeguard the freedom and dignity of all people, democracy must widen and deepen."[11]

The international community recognizes, through several declarations, that democracy is the preeminent system of governance; nevertheless, in various states, "the path to democratisation has proven tortuous; traditional and informal sources of power and authority vie for legitimacy, sometimes constituting an alternate 'state' within a state."[12] In post-reconstruction Afghanistan, for example, regional warlords have sought legitimisation by adopting the trappings of democracy.[13] Both Iraq and Afghanistan are illustrations of attempts at state building where success has been elusive, largely attributable to the realities on the ground in these countries. These examples have led policymakers to note that "[d]emocracy may be a good thing in itself, but it can only work where there is a functioning state to democratize."[14]

Institution building is critical to bringing about stability, and postconflict elections are an important step in the process of state reconstruction. Stability will be a major challenge facing the post-Karzai government, and if the country is to avoid a culture of impunity, respect rule of law, and put effort into reconstruction, then violent actors should not be brought into the process. As noted previously, there is a clear need to ensure that women hold positions of influence, as women in power are critical to the success of state building and any peace-building developments taking place after the April 5, 2014, presidential elections.

A 2013 report notes that nonmilitary spending by the United States in Afghanistan since 2002 "is approximately $100 billion,"15 with US Congress in appropriating another US$16.5 billion for reconstruction.[16] Additionally, other donor countries have spent billions on institution building, with some estimating that the external aid is running at around US$3 billion per year.

The challenges of reconstruction in Afghanistan are complex and multifaceted. Reconstruction is burdened at times by history and geography. Strategies require establishing transparent and accountable rule of law procedures, ending impunity, creating security, rebuilding the economy, and providing a greater role for women and minorities. During my visit to Afghanistan in 2010, Dr Jalal raised an important point: noting the billions of dollars that the international community was spending on Afghanistan's defence and reconstruction, could it not spend a few million on opening a women's television and radio channel?

Robert Rotberg argues that prevention and reconstruction of failed states requires "getting nation building right," which "is possible if there is sufficient political will and targeted external assistance."[17] Rotberg points to what is required of transitional administrations in order for them to become more effective in providing basic security, rebuilding the police forces, training national government administrators, promoting the rule of law, revitalizing economies, and even registering voters. He discusses the problems that arise from short-term fixes and advocates for more commitment:

> [S]ustainable nation building demands more than a quick fix. It requires a long-term commitment by outsiders to building capacities, strengthening security, and developing human resources. The uncomfortable but necessary lesson of these partially effective attempts is that the revival of failed states will prove more successful if a regional or international organisation takes charge

and only very gradually relinquishes authority to an indigenous transitional administration.[18]

Reconstruction efforts in Afghanistan will never succeed unless there are local partners who earnestly want to help strengthen the capacity of the state to provide positive services to their people, including good governance, rule of law, security, and an end to corruption.

Role of United Nations—UN Assistance Mission in Afghanistan

Long before Hamid Karzai's transition administration, the United Nations was looking at ways for the international community to put together a new peace-building architecture—a "central instrument for the prevention and resolution of conflicts and for the preservation of peace"[19]—in order to assist Afghanistan's transition from war to peace.

The Security Council and, to a lesser degree, the General Assembly[20] have put forth comprehensive resolutions regarding conflict prevention and peacekeeping, notwithstanding the frequent lack in political will throughout the international community to commit to peacekeeping operations and humanitarian assistance.[21] The Security Council recognised the urgency of the situation in Afghanistan following the overthrow of the Taliban and called for the United Front of Afghans representatives to "establish a new and transitional administration leading to the formation of a government"[22] that should "respect the human rights of all Afghan people, regardless of gender, ethnicity or religion...international obligations, including by cooperating fully in international efforts to combat terrorism and illicit drug trafficking."[23] The Council reaffirmed the central role for the United Nations in the establishment of the transitional administration and called on member states to provide support for such an endeavor.[24]

In March 2002, the UN Security Council adopted Resolution 1401 and established the UN Assistance Mission in Afghanistan to assist the people of Afghanistan in "laying the foundations for sustainable peace and development in the country."[25] Its mandate has been renewed annually, and on March 19, 2014, the Security Council adopted Resolution 2096 to authorize the Assistance Mission to focus on the organisation of the 2014 presidential elections.[26] Resolution 2096 reiterates Security Council support for Afghanistan's transition process and the importance of a comprehensive approach to address "security, economic, governance and development challenges, noting that these are of an interconnected nature, and recogniz[ing] that there is no 'purely military solution' to ensure the country's stability."[27] Secretary-General's Special Representative for Afghanistan Ján Kubiš announced in November 2013 that there were eleven Presidential candidates for the upcoming election.[28]

There are currently fifteen peacekeeping operations and one special political mission (UN Assistance Mission in Afghanistan). The International Security Assistance Force is a peacekeeping force under the framework that was set up at the initial Bonn Conference. Peacekeeping is generally defined as "a non-coercive instrument of diplomacy, where a legitimate, international civil and/or military coalition is employed with the consent of the belligerent parties, in an impartial, non-combatant manner, to implement conflict prevention and/or resolution arrangements or assist humanitarian aid operations."[29]

Peacebuilding "is a set of strategies, which aim to ensure that disputes, armed conflicts, and other major crises do not arise in the first place or if they do arise that they do not subsequently recur."[30] However, the boundaries of peacekeeping and peacebuilding have become increasingly blurred over time as missions are not always limited to one type of operation.[31]

Peacekeeping by the United Nations has evolved over the years and, with regard to the reconstruction of failed states, is an expensive undertaking. The Security Council has the legal and primary responsibility under the UN Charter to take collective action to maintain international peace and security, and to sanction peacekeeping operations. As noted above, the UN peacekeeping missions in postconflict failed states have been called upon to perform several tasks, and their mandate, as indicated by the United Nations, is to "maintain peace and security…facilitate the political process, protect civilians, assist in the disarmament, demobilisation and reintegration of former combatants; support the organisation of elections, protect and promote human rights and assist in restoring the rule of law."[32]

Notwithstanding the importance of peacekeeping, the term is hard to define and is not found in the UN Charter, although the authorisation is generally considered to fall between Chapter VI and Chapter VII. Dag Hammarskjöld, the second UN secretary-general, states that peacekeeping falls under "'Chapter VI and a half' of the Charter, somewhere between traditional methods of resolving disputes peacefully (outlined in Chapter VI), on the one hand, and more forceful, less 'consent-based' action (Chapter II)."[33]

Generally speaking, peacekeeping is designed to preserve the peace where fighting has been halted. It rests on three principles: consent of parties, impartiality, and nonuse of force, except in self-defense and defense of the mandate.[34] Peacekeeping by the United Nations is one among a range of measures undertaken to maintain international peace and security. Traditionally, these peacekeeping measures have generally been military in character and may involve "observation, monitoring and reporting."[35] Again, the general argument is that peacemaking generally involves diplomatic action and is facilitated by envoys and other actors to create conditions of a lasting settlement, while peacebuilding measures are intended to reduce the danger of relapsing into conflict by "strengthening national capacities for conflict management."[36] Peacebuilding and peacemaking have not been easy to implement in Afghanistan given the ongoing insurgency. Both the International Security Assistance Force and the UN Assistance Mission in Afghanistan were provided with a mandate authorised by the Security Council, but the lesson learned in Afghanistan is about the challenges of simultaneously fighting a war on terror and attempting peace building.

Humanitarian Assistance

The United Nations works with a range of partners, both governmental and nongovernmental, to provide humanitarian and developmental assistance in various international crises and complex emergencies. Since the adoption in 1991 of Resolution 46/182[37] by the General Assembly, the basic framework for humanitarian assistance has expanded considerably, reflecting both the broadening of the humanitarian effort not just in responding to natural disasters but also to the shifting environment in which assistance is offered in many failed states. The Security Council has stressed that states must respect the principles of international humanitarian law and cooperate during humanitarian operations, as such operations are complicated in areas of conflict.

The General Assembly adopted Resolution 46/182 in order to address the issue of humanitarian assistance and to provide guidelines based on the three core principles of humanity, neutrality, and impartiality.[38] Resolution 46/182 also emphasizes the importance of the sovereignty of states.[39]

Political will is imperative. Too often, the Security Council and the international community have failed to deliver according to expectations. Attempts by the United Nations to mobilize the international community to address various humanitarian disasters have not always met with a good outcome; in the case of Afghanistan, however, enormous financial investment continues. Unfortunately, accountability by the Karzai administration is lacking, and there is not much to show for the financial aid. As the International Crisis Group has noted in its report:

> [A]fter a decade of major security, development and humanitarian assistance, the international community has failed to achieve a politically stable and economically viable Afghanistan. Despite billions of dollars in aid, state institutions remain fragile and unable to provide good governance, deliver basic services to the majority of the population or guarantee human security.[40]

Early in the post-Taliban transition administration, the United States established the Provincial Reconstruction Teams to give the military a lead role in humanitarian reconstruction. Many of the positive initial achievements have been reversed by the insurgents who, along with killing civilians, have also destroyed many of the infrastructure projects that were constructed by the United States and its partners.

Notes

1. In *State Legitimacy and Failure in International Law* (BRILL, 2014), I note that there are ten broad categories by which to identify state failure. They encompass both the causes and the characteristics of failed states. These categories, which represent the essential areas of structural

competency, are as follows: (1) absence of rule of law, (2) political instability and lack of legitimacy, (3) economic and social instability directly contributing to poverty, (4) lack of security or the presence internal conflict, (5) authoritarian rule and clan loyalty, (6) impunity and an ineffective justice system, (7) loss of internal territorial control (de jure and de facto sovereignty), (8) gross and systematic violations of human rights, (9) loss of social cohesion and development and (10) corruption and a weak and ineffective bureaucracy.

2. Stephen M. Walt, "Beyond bin Laden: Reshaping U.S. Foreign Policy," International Security, Vol. 26, No. 3 (Winter 2001/02) at 62.
3. Lars Engberg-Pedersen et al, *Fragile States on the International Agenda,* Copenhagen: Danish Institute of International Studies (2008) at 11.
4. Stewart Patrick, "Weak States and Global Threats: Fact or Fiction?," *The Washington Quarterly,* Vol. 29, No. 2 (Spring 2006) at 37.
5. Elsina Wainwright, "Responding to state failure—the case of Australia and Solomon Islands," *Australian Journal of International Affairs,* Vol. 57, No. 3 (November 2003) at 486.
6. Afghan & the United Nations, UN News, 24 January 2014. Available at: http://www.un.org/News/dh/latest/afghan/un-afghanhistory.shtml
7. Erik Brattberg, Europe, Afghanistan and the Transatlantic Relationship after 2014, Stockholme International Peace Research Institute, May 2013.
8. "Governance for sustainable human development, Good governance - and sustainable human development," United Nations Development Programme, policy document, 1996.
9. Derick W. Brinkerfoff, "Rebuilding Governance in Failed States and Post-Conflict," *Public Administration and Development,* Vol. 25, No. 1, 2005 at 5.
10. *Human Development Report 2002: Deepening Democracy in a Fragmented World,* Oxford: Oxford University Press, 2002 at 2.
11. *Ibid.* at 1.
12. Derick W. Brinkerfoff, "Rebuilding Governance in Failed States and Post-Conflict," *Public Administration and Development,* Vol. 25, No. 1, 2005 at 5.
13. *Ibid.*
14. Lars Engberg-Pedersen et al, *Fragile Situations Background Papers,* Copenhagen: Danish Institute for International Studies, 2008 at 14–15.
15. "Money Pit: The Monstrous Failure of US Aid to Afghanistan," Joel Brinkley, World Affairs, January/February 2013. Available at:

    http://www.worldaffairsjournal.org/article/money-pit-monstrous-failure-us-aidafghanistan.
16. *Ibid.*

17. Robert I. Rotberg, "Failed States in a World of Terror," *Foreign Affairs,* Vol. 81, No.4, July/August 2002 at 127-140.
18. *Ibid.*
19. *An Agenda for Peace Preventive diplomacy, peacemaking and peackeeping,* New York: Report of the Secretary-General, 17 June 1992.
20. The General Assembly has put forward several declarations, including the *Manila Declaration on the Peaceful Settlement of International Disputes,* New York (15 November 1982) and the *Declaration on the Prevention and Removal of Disputes* and Situation Which May Threaten International Peace and Security and on the Role *of the United Nations in this Field,* 68th plenary meeting A/RES/43/51, 5 December 1998.
21. *An Agenda for Peace Preventive diplomacy, peacemaking and peace-keeping,* New York: Report of the Secretary-General, 17 June 1992.
22. "Security Council Sets United Nations Course for Supporting New Governance in Afghanistan; Urges No Reprisals

    Resolution 1378, Adopted Unanimously, Anticipates Broad-Based, Multi-Ethnic Transitional Administration, Leading to New Government", UN News, 14 November 2001. Available at: http://www.un.org/News/Press/docs/2001/sc7212.doc.htm
23. *Ibid.*
24. *Ibid.*
25. United Nations Assistance Mission in Afghanistan (UNAMA) is a political mission established by the Security Council in 2002 at the request of the Government to assist it and the people of Afghanistan in laying the foundations for sustainable peace and development in the country. More information available at:

    http://unama.unmissions.org/Default.aspx?tabid=12255&language=en-US
26. UN Security Council Resolution 2096, adopted at its 6935th meeting, on 19 March 2013. Available at:

    http://www.un.org/en/ga/search/view_doc.asp?symbol=S/RES/2096(2013)
27. Afghan in Brief, Embassy of Afghanistan, Washington DC, 24 January 2014.
28. "UNAMA welcomes final list of candidates for 2014 Afghan elections," UNAMA Press Statement, 20 November 2013.
29. Peace Operations: An Australian Perspective, Commonwealth of Australia, 2009. Available at: http://www.defence.gov.au/adfwc/peacekeeping/terminology.htm
30. *Ibid.*
31. Peace and Security, United Nations Peacekeeping available at:

    http://www.un.org/en/peacekeeping/operations/peace.shtml
32. United Nation Peacekeeping website, available at:

    http://www.un.org/en/peacekeeping/

33. *Ibid.*
34. *United Nations Peacekeeping Operations, Principles and Guidelines,* New York: Department of Peacekeeping Operations (2010) at 31.
35. *Ibid.* at 21.
36. *Ibid.* at 25.
37. General Assembly Resolution 46/182, 19 December 1991.
38. *Guidelines on The Use of Military and Civil Defence Assets To Support United Nations Humanitarian Activities in Complex Emergencies,* document developed with the collaboration of a broad representation of the international humanitarian community, through a Drafting Committee consisting of representatives of Austria, Czech Republic, France, Germany, Italy, Sudan, Switzerland, UK, USA, DPKO, SCHR, UNHCR, UNICEF and WFP, as well as a Review Committee consisting of representatives of Australia, Canada, China, Costa Rica, Denmark, Ecuador, Egypt, Estonia, Finland, Ghana, Greece, India, Japan, Libyan Arab Jamahiriya, Madagascar, Mauritius, Mexico, Netherlands, Norway, Poland, Russian Federation, Sweden, Turkey, Yugoslavia, COE, ECHO, EC, EUMS, ICDO, ICRC, ICVA, INTERACTION, IOM, NATO, OCHA, THW and WHO, March 2003 at 8.
39. *Ibid.* at 8.
40. http://www.crisisgroup.org/en/regions/asia/south-asia/afghanistan/210-aid-andconflict- in-afghanistan.aspx

Chapter 3

Application of International Law

Humanitarian Intervention

The legality of humanitarian intervention depends in great part upon who is interpreting the conventions. Legal realists endeavor to justify humanitarian intervention in Afghanistan through a liberal understanding of Chapter VII, Article 39: Action with Respect to Threats to the Peace, Breaches of the Peace, and Acts of Aggression, which states that the "Security Council shall determine the existence of any threat to the peace, breach of the peace, or act of aggression and shall make recommendations, or decide what measures shall be taken in accordance with Articles 41 and 42, to maintain or restore international peace and security."[1] Legal realists argue that Article 39 gives the Security Council "jurisdiction over any 'threat to the peace,' rather than over any threat to international peace, therefore permitting it to intervene in order to end human rights violations that lack trans-boundary effects."[2]

Notwithstanding the legal obligations of the Security Council to act when there is a threat to peace, its actions have had, to date, mixed success. During the civil war in the early 1990s in Somalia, the international community became alarmed by the spiral of violence and state failure. On December 3, 1992, the Security Council unanimously adopted Resolution 794, which "strongly condemned the violations of international law and demanded the cessation of all hostilities from all parties involved."[3] The Security Council further determined that the civil war was a threat to international peace and security, which was "further exacerbated by the obstacles being created to the distribution of humanitarian assistance."[4]

It has been argued by several legal scholars that the Genocide Convention, by enjoining its signatories to "prevent and punish" the "crime of genocide," may have made genocide the exceptional circumstance that warrants intervention.[5] Many states are signatories to international treaties that recognize the fundamental respect for human rights, and most legal scholars would argue that the prohibitions on genocide and crimes against humanity are essential to the maintenance of an international legal order.

The notion of use of force that violates the territorial integrity or political independence of a state for the purpose of humanitarian intervention is in the early stages of debate and may, over time, come to be considered as a customary norm supported by the majority of states. It should also be noted that the development of customary international law has long been a matter of debate and disagreement among legal scholars and states, especially the notion concerning state practice.[6]

Several legal scholars, such as Thomas Franck, note that international law "has begun gingerly to develop ways to bridge the gap between what is requisite in strict legality and what is generally regarded as just and moral."[7] India's intervention in East Pakistan in 1971 in reaction to Pakistan's immense human right violations, the Tanzanian 1979 intervention in Uganda (which led to the overthrow of the dictatorial and murderous regime of Idi Amin), and the Vietnamese intervention in 1978 against Pol Pot's genocidal regime in Cambodia have all been alluded to as humanitarian interventions in response to human rights violations, yet all were all without UN Security Council approval.[8]

In this regard, the linkage between violations of human rights and international armed conflicts that pose a threat to international peace and security could provide a space in which humanitarian intervention would be possible. Serious violations of human rights in failed states create inroads in the traditional perceptions of state sovereignty,[9] leading some scholars, such as Alexandros Yannis, to suggest that there has been a shift away from state-centred consideration towards the individual.[10] However, even states that have intervened in order to end dreadful human rights abuses have been reluctant to invoke a customary right of unauthorised humanitarian intervention to defend their actions. India's justification of its invasion of East Pakistan was self-defense, Vietnam argued that it was reacting to an aggressive war, and Tanzania defended its actions as a response to Uganda's invasion of Kagera.[11]

There is an emerging practice based on the responsibility of human protection. This fundamental principle is contained in the International Commission on Intervention and State Sovereignty report and in the Security Council's evolving interpretation of what constitutes a threat to international peace and security.[12] A number of legal sources provide a framework for the emerging principle, which favors military intervention in situations where human protection is required. The International Commission on Intervention and State Sovereignty argues that there should be increased flexibility when considering military intervention, in spite of the Charter's predisposition against such action.[13] Several world leaders who have spoken before the UN General Assembly have argued in favor of the doctrine of the Responsibility to Protect.[14] The Secretary-General Ban Ki-moon also stressed the importance of this principle, noting that "this doctrine has gone from crawling to walking to running...Let us do our utmost to ensure that this umbrella of protection covers all who need it."[15]

Much debate has arisen around the central question of what form the response of the world community should take in the face of state failure where gross violations of human rights are occurring. Does the international community have a responsibility to act? In failed states, such as Afghanistan during the Taliban rule, where administrative institutions have collapsed, provisions for human rights are largely ineffective, terrorist activities are widespread, and safe havens are being provided with the state offering no more than peripheral protection to its people.[16]

The International Commission on Intervention and State Sovereignty, in its "Responsibility to Protect" report, advanced the notion of "sovereignty as responsibility." The report was release at the same time that the worst terrorist attack on the United States took place on September 1, 2001. The notion of responsibility to protect was first introduced by Francis Deng, at the Brookings Institution in 1996, and challenged the established principle of absolute state sovereignty that recognised the sovereignty of a state regardless of whether that state committed serious human rights abuses against its own citizens.[17]

The Commission further added to the debate over what should be done if a state fails and is unable or unwilling to stop gross and systematic violations of human rights, by noting that "if states do not live up to their responsibilities, it is the task of the more responsible members of the international community to intervene – for the sake not only of the beleaguered citizens, but also of wider international peace and security."[18]

The report, while addressing the issue of humanitarian intervention, has left many other issues unresolved. International law codifies the doctrine of nonintervention as enshrined in the UN Charter which prohibits nations from attacking other states. Article 2(4) stipulates that all members "shall refrain in their international relations from the threat or use of force against the territorial integrity or political independence of any state, or in any other manner inconsistent with the Purposes of the United Nations."[19]

However, it should be noted that Article 51 of the Charter states that "[n]othing in the present Charter shall impair the inherent right of individual or collective self-defence if an armed attack occurs against a Member of the United Nations." Also, the Security Council may authorize the use of force under Chapter VII in order to maintain or restore international peace and security.

However, many legal scholars, including Professor Michael Reisman of Yale Law School, have made the argument that states cannot be expected to remain idle while a great number of people die; the Charter was not a suicide pact.[20] The principle of the Responsibility to Protect appeared in the High Level Panel report in 2004 and in Secretary General Kofi Annan's 2005 report "Larger Freedom," and was approved at the High Panel plenary meeting of the sixtieth session of the General Assembly in October 2005.

Protecting human rights and respecting the emerging norms of humanitarian intervention require concrete definitions, thus some legal scholars have looked to the criteria set out in the doctrine of the Responsibility to Protect for humanitarian intervention to provide answers to unresolved questions. For example, the Responsibility to Protect report declares that there is no "better or more appropriate body than the UN Security Council to authorize military intervention for human protection purposes."[21]

The Responsibility to Protect advances the notion that state sovereignty is a privilege and not a right, and is derived from a reciprocal relationship of respect between the state and its citizens.[22] At the 2005 World Summit, the UN General Assembly agreed that if a state is unwilling or unable to protect its own citizens against gross and systematic violations of internationally recognised human rights, the international community must assume the responsibility to protect them. Under such circumstances, the international community has a duty to launch preventative, reactive, and rebuilding measures that are aimed at protecting defenseless civilians from abuse by their own governments. The "UN General Assembly World Summit Outcome Document" singled out prevention as the most important element of the Responsibility to Protect. In addition, there is growing belief in sovereignty as an evolving principle, intrinsically linked to the security and protection of civilians.[23]

Notwithstanding the need for a paradigm shift that will persuade states to adopt the concept of state failure prevention as outlined previously, the reality is simply that the arguments in favor of the doctrine of Responsibility to Protect have been used by some states inconsistently. The advancing notion is that ignoring weak and failed states invariably leads to serious atrocities and civil conflict, and poses both national and international threats. The Responsibility to Protect doctrine is just one tool that can be used by states and the international community in dealing with failed states. However, dealing with failed states will of course require a broad spectrum of tools, including soft and hard power and, essentially, the political will of the international community.

The Charter gives the Security Council authority to act; however, the debate surrounding the legality of intervention when it takes place outside of a United Nations mandate (e.g., Iraq) is much more complicated. The shift is away from the state and the focus is on the victims; people suffering violence and human rights abuses. However, the responsibility to protect one's population is still the primary due of the government, and only in the absence or failure to act is the international community bound to act.

The use of military force against another state with the aim of ending grave human rights violations continues to be the subject of much debate in the realm of public international law. Along with fighting against the terrorist threat to peace and security, several nations justified their actions in Afghanistan based on human rights violations against women. There is no one, standard legal definition of humanitarian intervention.

Most legal scholars would prefer that the Security Council take action under Chapter VII of the Charter and respond during humanitarian emergencies that constitute a threat to peace. The Security Council has broadened its interpretation of the Charter to include use of force in situations that are actually internal conflicts. Several arguments have surfaced justifying the new rules governing the use of force; however, to date there is no consensus on an emergence of a new customary law.

The Vienna Declaration, proclaiming the universal, indivisible, interdependent, and interrelated character of human rights, was unanimously adopted by all UN member states that were present, along with the recognition that the gap between rhetoric and reality needs to be bridged. This challenge is complicated by the daily litany of violations of human rights by several states. The predicament has led policy makers and legal scholars to advocate for humanitarian intervention in order to prevent gross and systematic violations of human rights. The use of force in international law in order to stop a humanitarian catastrophe is multifaceted in its characterisation and implementation, and is highly controversial when carried out without Security Council Chapter VII approval.

Humanitarian intervention has generated much discussion as a consequence of both the post–cold war era debate surrounding human rights at the international level and the growing understanding of the relationship between international security and violations of human rights. The international legal scholar Fernando Teson puts forward the liberal argument of humanitarian intervention as the "proportionate international use or threat of military force, undertaken in principle by a liberal government or alliance, aimed at ending tyranny or anarchy, welcomed by the victims, and consistent with the doctrine of double effect."[24]

The doctrine of double effect has its origins in the works of Saint Thomas Aquinas on the ethical and moral criteria for evaluating the permissibility of certain acts.[25] For Teson, human rights must prevail, and the international legal system must be changed to allow for the implementation of human rights standards, even if this means overriding conventional international law.

In the case of Afghanistan, the Security Council did take action against the territorial integrity and political independence of the state, but in accordance with the UN Charter and with the backing of international law.

Transitional Occupation in Afghanistan

The shift from the classical notion of belligerent occupation to the endorsement of "transformative occupation" that is sanctioned by the world community comes with political risk, as the occupant must create conditions under which a new political order can be established and legitimized under international law. Generally speaking, most states accept the customary international law principle that prohibits a unilateral annexation of a given territory. It was understandable therefore that the development of *occupatio bellum* as a legal institution was a subject of significant debate when the United States and its allies took military control of Afghanistan and Iraq. At the time of the Iraq invasion, several legal arguments for its "legality" were advanced based on the notion of "preventive self-defense," but today most legal scholars question whether the invasion met the legal threshold under international law.

International administration of a territory—such as East Timor and Kosovo, where the United Nations forces were endowed with wide-ranging executive, administrative, and legislative powers— was not exercised in subsequent missions in Afghanistan and Iraq. In Afghanistan, the United States had a clear transformative purpose; the US-led military coalition was aimed explicitly at deposing the ruling regime. However, after the fall of the Taliban, the coalition's role was essentially to aid the Afghan Interim Authority in implementing political, social, and economic change.

Legal scholars have struggled with the current public international law framework concerning the legitimacy of transitional occupation to construct conditions for social reform. Humanitarian law regulates the powers of an occupant and the limits of military conduct. However, the ability of transformative occupation to change a failed state to achieve structural competency and a series of legitimate transformative policies need to be examined. This examination should take place not just in the in the context of the humanitarian law development of the present Hague Regulation and the Fourth Geneva Convention that regulate conduct of war (*jus in bello*) but also in the context of human rights and the net benefits to the local populations during periods of transformational occupations.

The notion of military intervention with a transformative purpose must be considered by the international community if it is going to have some form of shared sovereignty in managing the daily internal affairs of a failing state. The United Nations can have a key role in legitimizing the role of an occupying power.

Whether under the international law framework the occupying power has the legal right to establish conditions for a democratic and peaceful transition as well as to introduce fundamental changes to the state is a question that was addressed in part by Resolution 1483 of the Security Council when it revisited the notion of *occupatio bellum*. *Jus in bello*, as understood in international humanitarian law, governs the conduct of warfare and places limits on the suffering that may be caused by war. This is independent from *jus ad bellum* questions about the justification for war. However, there is much debate as to whether there are persuasive arguments that Resolution 1483 derogated from the core principles of international law. The law of occupation as established under international humanitarian law is primarily embodied in the Fourth Geneva Convention (1949) and the Hague Regulations (1907),[26] which the Security Council noted in Resolution 1483, and they present a deposit of principles governing the conduct of the occupying power during the period that it is in control of territory that is not its own.

These regulations were designed to have an important role in the conduct of the occupying power. Although, since the end of colonialism and the Cold War, most states do not wish to be perceived as occupying powers—notwithstanding the fact that there have been other examples of military intervention sanctioned by the UN Security Council, including Afghanistan, Cambodia, Bosnia-Herzegovina, Haiti, Kosovo, and East Timor. In each case, measures were taken by several Security Council resolutions to establish international administrations that exercised some degree of shared sovereignty over the territories in question.[27]

In the case of Afghanistan, NATO, and particularly the United States as an occupying power, had a clear transitional occupation role that was legally sanctioned by the United Nations. Resolution 1386 was adopted unanimously on December 20, 2011, and, under Chapter VII of the Charter of the UN mandate, authorised the contribution of military and other resources by member states to the International Security Assistance Force and called upon the people of Afghanistan to "cooperate with the International Security Assistance Force and relevant international governmental and nongovernmental organisations."[28]

Application of International Law: Non-State Actors

The frameworks of both international humanitarian law and international human rights law govern the international armed conflict between the US and NATO forces and insurgency groups such as the Taliban, Al Qaeda, the Haqqani network, Hezb-e-Islami. Given these groups are nontraditional combatants in an armed conflict of a noninternational character who nevertheless can project their influence globally poses several challenges to existing legal norms.

Following 9/11, the terms "unlawful combatants" and "enemy combatant" began to be widely employed by the United States for those suspected with ties to Al Qaeda and who were deemed by the United States as not qualifying for prisoner of war status under the Geneva Conventions. In addition, Al Qaeda members belong to a transnational organisation with operational cells in several states. Both the White House interpretation of the Geneva Conventions relating to prisoner of war status and the employment of the term "unlawful combatants" were widely criticized by most international human rights institutions. Eventually, during President Obama's administration, the term was abandoned in 2009; however, many questions surrounding nonstate actors remain unresolved in international law.

International law recognizes as lawful the armed conflict of states as long as they respect international humanitarian law. Those captured during hostilities are entitled to prisoner of war status.[29] The situation becomes murkier when dealing with failed states or with terrorists who can operate in a host of countries with the intent of targeting civilian populations. In these situations, a state may not be involved in the hostilities. Today's "noninternational" armed conflicts are for the most part transnational in nature, straddling several states despite only one state being involved in the fighting. In response to the confusion in the use of the terms such as "unlawful combatants," the International Committee of the Red Cross provided a legal advisor, who stated that from an international humanitarian law perspective

> the term "combatant" or "enemy combatant" has no legal meaning outside of armed conflict. To the extent that persons designated "enemy combatants" have been captured in international or non-international armed conflict, the provisions and protections of international humanitarian law remain applicable regardless of how such persons are called. Similarly, when individuals are captured outside of armed conflict their actions and protection are governed by domestic law and human rights law, regardless of how they are called."[30]

International humanitarian law clearly defines the terms "combatant," "prisoner of war," and "civilian;" the confusion, however, lies in the terms "unlawful combatants" and "unprivileged combatants/

belligerents" and to what extent these people are involved in armed conflicts. These questions are not dealt with in international treaties. Since 9/11, the jurisprudence on the topic of "unlawful combatant" and what constitutes an armed conflict has evolved. A key contribution was the October 2, 1995, decision of the International Criminal Tribunal for the Former Yugoslavia[31] in the case of *Prosecutor v. Tadic*, Appeal on Jurisdiction, which held that

> armed conflict exists whenever there is a resort to armed force between States or protracted armed violence between such groups within a State. International humanitarian law applies from the initiation of such conflicts and extends beyond the cessation of hostilities until a general conclusion of peace is reached; or, in the case of internal armed conflicts, a peaceful settlement is achieved. Until that moment, international humanitarian law continues to apply in the whole territory of the warring States or, in the case of internal conflicts, the whole territory under the control of a party, whether or not actual combat takes place there.[32]

The Tribunal's definition does not require that armed groups exercise control over territory within the state: "In defining the territorial field of application for internal armed conflicts, the tribunal only makes clear that humanitarian law applies (1) even in territory no longer under the control of the state; and (2) throughout such territory."[33]

In addition, the Third Geneva Convention regulates the obligation to give prisoner of war status to "[m]embers of regular armed forces who profess allegiance to a government or an authority not recognised by the Detaining Power."[34] Both Common Article 3 and Additional Protocol II apply to armed conflicts and not to sporadic acts of violence such as riots. The Geneva Convention did not envision this type of conflict or the phenomena of failing states being havens for terrorist cells. An effort to arrive at a general definition of noninternational armed conflict was attempted under Protocol II of the Geneva Convention, which was adopted on June 8, 1977, and entered into force on December 7, 1978.[35] Protocol II resolves many unclear issues surrounding the definition of armed conflict in Common Article 3 of the Geneva Convention. Afghanistan ratified Protocol II on November 10, 2009, which entered into force on December 24, 2009. The Protocol prohibits attacks against civilians and acts or threats of violence whose primary purpose is to spread terror among the civilian population. Afghanistan has also ratified the Rome Statute of the International Criminal Court in 2003.[36] The United States is not a party to Protocols I and II, and the Rome Statute.

Lawful combatants when captured under international humanitarian law are to be treated as prisoners of war (POW); however, an unlawful combatant under Geneva Convention III, Article 4, does not qualify for POW status:

A. Prisoners of war, in the sense of the present Convention, are persons belonging to one of the following categories, who have fallen into the power of the enemy:

1. Members of the armed forces of a Party to the conflict as well as members of militias or volunteer corps forming part of such armed forces.
2. Members of other militias and members of other volunteer corps, including those of organised resistance movements, belonging to a Party to the conflict and operating in or outside their own territory, even if this territory is occupied, provided that such militias or volunteer corps, including such organised resistance movements, fulfill the following conditions:
   (a) That of being commanded by a person responsible for his subordinates;
   (b) That of having a fixed distinctive sign recognizable at a distance;
   (c) That of carrying arms openly;
   (d) That of conducting their operations in accordance with the laws and customs of war.
3. Members of regular armed forces who profess allegiance to a government or an authority not recognised by the Detaining Power.
4. Persons who accompany the armed forces without actually being members thereof, such as civilian members of military aircraft crews, war correspondents, supply

contractors, members of labour units or of services responsible for the welfare of the armed forces, provided that they have received authorisation from the armed forces which they accompany, who shall provide them for that purpose with an identity card similar to the annexed model.

5. Members of crews [of civil ships and aircraft], who do not benefit by more favorable treatment under any other provisions of international law.
6. Inhabitants of a non-occupied territory, who on the approach of the enemy spontaneously take up arms to resist the invading forces, without having had time to form themselves into regular armed units, provided they carry arms openly and respect the laws and customs of war.[37]

Thus, the Third Geneva Convention divides combatants in an armed conflict into two categories—those in armies and organised militias and those who are not. The protection afforded to lawful combatants is not the same as that afforded to unlawful combatants. Individuals protected by the Fourth Convention and Protocol I

> may be prosecuted under domestic law for directly participating in hostilities. They may be interned for as long as they pose a serious security threat, and, while in detention, may under specific conditions be denied certain privileges under the Fourth Geneva Convention. They may also be prosecuted for war crimes and other crimes and sentenced to terms exceeding the length of the conflict, including the range of penalties provided for under domestic law.[38]

Nonetheless, individual who are not covered by either the Third or the Fourth Geneva Conventions are entitled to the fundamental guarantees provided for by customary international law relating to conditions of treatment and due process of law.

Universal Jurisdiction

Universal jurisdiction is a principle whereby states assert jurisdiction over persons who are alleged to have committed crimes outside the boundaries of the prosecuting state.[39] This trend has increased with the emergence of many failed states. As the secretary-general noted:

> Universal jurisdiction involved a criterion for the attribution of jurisdiction, whereas the obligation to extradite or prosecute was an obligation that was discharged once the accused was extradited or once the state decided to prosecute an accused based on any of the existing bases of jurisdiction.[40]

Universal jurisdiction is asserted by the state and therefore is distinguished from the jurisdiction exercised by an international tribunal.

The principle of universal jurisdiction has been extensively debated in the cases of prosecuted individuals from failing states who have been sheltered by weak impunity laws and against whom the state has failed to take action. Several leading human rights organisations are campaigning in favor of empowering states to enact legislation that would provide a universal jurisdiction mechanism to investigate and prosecute perpetrators and to use national courts to bring them to justice, regardless of where the crime was committed. Some, however, have argued that the creation of the International Criminal Court has reduced the need for national courts to apply the doctrine of universal jurisdiction.

Nonetheless, there are many successful cases of states exercising universal jurisdiction in denying refugee status to individuals who have committed human rights violations outside their territory. Article 1F of the 1954 Refugee Convention renders an asylum seeker ineligible for refugee status if he or she has committed a "crime against peace, a war crime, or a crime against humanity" or a "serious non-political crime."[41] Several European countries have successfully applied universal jurisdiction by even going so far as undertaking extraterritorial investigations to collect evidence from abroad to bring perpetrators to justice.[42] In October 2005, two Afghan perpetrators were condemned to twelve and nine years of imprisonment by Dutch courts for their involvement in war crimes and torture in Afghanistan.[43]

The US-Afghan Bilateral Security Agreement would "provide the U.S. exclusive criminal jurisdiction over its service members for their criminal acts in Afghanistan."[44] Fundamentally, the current framework would remain in place. The Afghanistan administration has previously waived jurisdiction over US Army personnel; given the current dysfunctional and corrupt Afghan legal system, it is understandable why the United States would want to maintain that arrangement. Ultimately, Afghanistan will have to balance imposed constraints on sovereignty with the security and development afforded them by the United States.

Despite the move to broaden the application of the principle of universal jurisdiction, the exercise of universal jurisdiction is not uniformly applied. In the 2002 International Court of Justice's decision in the *Case Concerning the Arrest Warrant of April 11, 2000* (Democratic Republic of the Congo v. Belgium), the Court judged that

> the issue and international circulation by Belgium of the arrest warrant of 11 April 2000 against Abdulaye Yerodia Ndombasi failed to respect the immunity from criminal jurisdiction and the inviolability which the incumbent Minister for Foreign Affairs of the Congo enjoyed under international law; and that Belgium must cancel the arrest warrant.[45]

Belgium had a legal obligation to issue an arrest warrant following parliamentary approval of the law of universal jurisdiction in 1993, when it issued an arrest warrant for the incumbent Minister for Foreign Affairs of the Democratic Republic of Congo (who was accused of war crimes involvement in the 1994 Rwandan genocide). The Democratic Republic of Congo challenged the warrant before the International Court of Justice, which rendered a favorable judgment. The judgment was a setback to jurisprudence concerning universal jurisdiction and to the crackdown on impunity.

The Rome Statute, which established the treaty of the International Criminal Court (ICC), entered into force on 1 July 1, 2002,46and it established four core international crimes under the jurisdiction of the ICC: genocide, crimes against humanity, war crimes, and the crime of aggression. The ICC will act when the relevant states are "unwilling" or "unable" to do so themselves. This development was a major one in the field of universal jurisdiction and in the push to end perpetrators' impunity from the law.

Article 27 of the Rome Statute conflicts with the 2002 International Court of Justice decision in that the latter does not recognize the immunity of states' officials under international law:

> 27.1 This Statute shall apply equally to all persons without any distinction based on official capacity. In particular, official capacity as a Head of State or Government, a member of a Government or parliament, an elected representative or a government official shall in no case exempt a person from criminal responsibility under this Statute, nor shall it, in and of itself, constitute a ground for reduction of sentence.
>
> 27.2. Immunities or special procedural rules which may attach to the official capacity of a person, whether under national or international law, shall not bar the Court from exercising its jurisdiction over such a person.[47]

Both humanitarian intervention and the introduction of the ICC have been controversial additions to the international legal system. In the case of the ICC, much controversy has centered on the cost, long delays, and focus on Africa; however, four out of eight ongoing ICC cases were referred by African governments.48The Court faces many challenges; however, notwithstanding these challenges, the ICC is an important step forward in international law; in particular, as regards universal jurisdiction and the pursuit of justice.

Afghanistan ratified the Rome Statute on February 10, 2003, and leading national and international human rights organisations have called for the Afghan government to cooperate with the ICC and to investigate all parties who have committed war crimes and crimes against humanity, especially insurgent groups who have deliberately targeted civilians.

Trusteeship-Limited Sovereignty

As with transitional occupation, the transferal of control by failed states to the United Nations Trusteeship Council requires considerable debate and a clear consensus among UN member states so as to prevent equating transferral of control with any form of colonial takeover. The trusteeship system is the successor of the League of Nations' mandate system and was principally established to help territories that did not have any form of self-government and were former mandates of the League of Nations before becoming independent countries. In 1994, with the newly independent Palau joining the United Nations, the Trusteeship Council was suspended.

As in the days of the mandate system, issues of state sovereignty and self-determination remain, with legal challenges to prospective trusteeships. The nature of the problems has changed somewhat. At the time the League of Nations was formed, sovereignty was an issue of concern, both because a Eurocentric understanding of international law aimed at excluding "uncivilised" nations from the definition of a sovereign state and because it was unclear who held sovereignty over mandated territories.[49]

The issue of trusteeship is today both complicated and political. Under the UN Trusteeship System, no member can be put under trusteeship due to the international legal principle of state sovereignty. Both the Security Council and the International Court of Justice have shown flexibility in their interpretation of the Charter, and the Security Council could authorize some form of shared sovereignty for assisting failed states to rebuild and become self-determining states. Nele Matz points out that

> [e]ven the UN Trusteeship System did not seem to find a conflict between self-determination and governance by an Administering Authority, since it appears that in accordance with Article 76 lit. b. of the Charter a right to selfdetermination is held in suspension until the Administering Authority has created circumstances that allow for its exercise. In contrast thereto, however, one might understand the right to self-determination to be an obstacle to political trusteeship, at least if the relevant people do not chose a political status that allows for assistance in a transitional period.[50]

The UN Charter must set out specific conventions if it is to ever move forward towards some form of shared sovereignty after state failure. A partnership needs to be encouraged between the United Nations and the member state, and trust needs to be developed at the local level to avoid any resentment by the population.

Under Chapter XII of the UN Charter, Articles 75–91 outline the authority of the International Trusteeship System. Under Article 75, for example, the "United Nations shall establish under its authority an international trusteeship system for the administration and supervision of such territories as may be placed there under by subsequent individual agreements. These territories are hereinafter referred to as trust territories."[51]

Chapter XII also outlines the terms for administration and designates authority as well as the procedures necessary for the establishment of the Trusteeship Council. It has been suggested that the notion of sovereign equality was unquestionably important to the architecture of the Charter following the devastation of the Second World War; however, at the time of signing there were only fifty-one member states of the United Nations, with only three being from Africa (Ethiopia, Liberia, and the Union of South Africa), as the rest were still under colonial rule.

On the question of failed states becoming part of a trusteeship, the secretary-general replied that this is something that member states of the United Nations will have to discuss.[52] The UN Charter would preclude the kind of trusteeship indicated above, as the International Trusteeship system applies only to former League mandates, territories captured during the Second World War, and other areas placed under trusteeship by their administering states. However, as stated in Article 78, "[t]he trusteeship system shall not apply to territories which have become Members of the United Nations."[53] This limitation reflects the colonial situation and the priorities of member states at the close of the Second World War. The creation of a trusteeship in 1945 over a member state would have been viewed as inconsistent with the premise that the United Nations was to be based upon "the principle of the sovereign equality of all Members"[54] and that it would not interfere with their internal affairs. However, states could voluntarily relinquish control over their internal and external affairs for a defined period of time. The trusteeship plan could go further than the Cambodia model, with the United Nations and the affected state becoming parties to a trusteeship agreement and either the United Nations or a group of states serving as the administering authority.[55]

Obtaining political consensus is a difficult undertaking at the United Nations, and changing the Charter would be even more challenging as many states would bring objections that such an action would undermine Article 2(1) or the "sovereign equality" provision. But, as noted by several scholars, most failed states hardly govern themselves, and thus the notion of sovereignty is changing.

UN resources are always an issue, as the Cambodia operation—the closest case to UN management of a sovereign state—perfectly exemplifies, with a cost exceeding US$1.6 billion during its two-year duration in a country of only eight million people.56 But, as illustrated above, the failure to act also has a high price, and the United Nations has the legal authority to act.

UN actions in the emerging states of Bosnia and the Democratic Republic of Timor-Leste require some level of compromised sovereignty. Bosnia had strong European support, while in the case of Timor-Leste, Australia took the leading role. The Westphalia system's traditional fundamental principles of legitimacy rest on the notion of state sovereignty; most failed states are unable to meet the demands of sovereignty.

The debate as to the best possible means of reconstructing a failed state is an ongoing one, and the proposal that sovereignty can be breached by outsiders in order to build the states can, for some, evoke disturbing images of colonialism. However, as noted above, there is a growing body of literature arguing that "international engagement must be more robust."[57] Nonetheless, the "idea that it might become a permanent or recurrent feature of international life is instinctively felt to be dangerous, since it undermines the principle of sovereign equality on which the current international is based."[58]

To improve the likelihood of successful reconstruction, a process that engages the indigenous population is always the one most desired. Nonetheless, although an imposed solution for reconstruction is not the preferred option, it may be needed if all else fails. Some scholars have indicated that a "certain degree of international control and imposition is necessary in order to bring about a well functioning state in which the ruling elite are accountable to the people."[59] In this context, the need to reintroduce a formal trusteeship that can ensure both accountability to agreements and delivery of results is being seriously debated.[60]

Michael Ignatieff argues that to fix failed states, sovereignty and the concept and practice of neutrality need to be rethought.[61] State failure in many parts of the world has its roots in weak state capacity. Ignatieff and other members of the International Commission on Intervention and State Sovereignty argue that the issues that arise when sovereignty is suspended during the period of intervention cannot be restored "unless the intervener has authority over a territory. But the suspension of the exercise of sovereignty is only *de facto* for the period of the intervention and follow-up, and not *de jure*."[62] For example, the Paris Accords of October 23, 1991, on Cambodia allowed for a comprehensive settlement, giving the United Nations effective authority to supervise a ceasefire, disarm the factional armies, and prepare the country for general elections. The objective of the Paris Accords was implemented through the Supreme National Council, with comprised representatives of the four competing factions and shared sovereignty with the United Nations. It has been suggested that, similarly, Yugoslavia "temporarily had its sovereignty over Kosovo suspended, though it has not lost it *de jure*."[63]

The settlement negotiation of Namibia provides a good example of UN trusteeship in the period of transition that led to its independence, with several legal classifications and compromises, in fact *sui generis*, of the UN operation:

> [T]he *de facto* but illegal occupying Power, South Africa, and the United Nations, in which *de jure* authority reposed but which had not previously been able to establish effective administration in Namibia, were to work together to enable the Namibian people to exercise their right of self-determination.[64]

The United Nations had a supervisory central objective, which was to hold free and fair elections for a constituent assembly that would draft a constitution leading to the independence of Namibia.[65] Some scholars have commented that the UN Trusteeship System "is to some extent a victim of its own success."[66]

Other notable scholars, such as Helman and Ratner, have argued for a return of the trusteeship model as a solution to failing states and recommend

> direct U.N. trusteeship when there is a total breakdown of governmental authority...the theoretical basis for conservatorship in the domestic analogue of the polity helping those who are utterly incapable of functioning on their own, thereby necessitating a legal regime where the community itself manages the affairs of the victim.[67]

Helman and Ratner recommend conservatorship as the theoretical paradigm for UN assistance to failed states. Helman and Ratner as well as Richard Caplan argued that it might be necessary to establish a trusteeship under the United Nations in extreme cases of state failure.[68] Caplan, for example, analyzed the transitional administration of Bosnia, Kosovo, and East Timor and noted that in each case the international community assumed responsibility for the governance of territories to a degree unprecedented in history.

These scholars would propose that the states in question "would voluntarily relinquish control."[69] This task is difficult but not impossible if there is political will on all sides. Stephen Krasner notes that to improve the well-being of the domestic population and decrease the threat to the international community, alternative options such as *de facto* trusteeships should be considered.[70] Krasner advances the notion of shared sovereignty involving the participation of external actors to assist with failed state reconstruction.[71] James Fearon and David Laitin[72] have argued for the establishment of neotrusteeship over divided postwar failed states. This arrangement or partnership would be voluntary and could be established by treaty for a limited period of time.[73] They also note that failed states have limited structural competency and are often unable to assist themselves.[74]

There are also numerous examples in which states under reconstruction use international administrations or external actors to assist them in running certain bureaucracies and programs, such as Bosnia under the terms of the Dayton Accords, Timor-Leste under the UN Transitional Administration, and Kosovo under the UN Interim Administration.75 In the case of Afghanistan and Iraq, security has been provided in large part by foreign forces.[76] *De facto* trusteeship or shared sovereignty, although not the panacea to the reconstruction of failed states, should be considered by local governments and the international community as a possible means by which to assist them in building a functional state.

Much of the debate is on the legal, moral, and practical implications of such large state-building mechanisms. Trusteeship reflects both the severity of the predicament and the challenge confronting policymakers and scholars regarding failed states. For these reasons scholars are today looking at trusteeship as a possible solution that is more comprehensive and more durable than other possible solutions.

The international community must pay more attention to the structural competencies of troubled states prior to their emergence as failing or failed states. To do so requires considerable resources and significant political will. The effectiveness of this approach can be compromised by a lack of consensus in the international community and of acceptable standards when measuring state failure.

There is also an incumbent responsibility on the part a trusteeship partner to work with local authorities and groups, which is, of course, a significant challenge. An example of the scope of this challenge is to be found in Afghanistan, where many would argue that the greatest beneficiaries of external intervention have been societal elites in the country.

It is time to replace the Westphalian concept of state sovereignty. By encompassing the universal principles of legitimacy, accountability, respect for human rights, and the rule of law, it is possible to attain political, social, and economic stability; in other words, the construction of states that are effective, capable, stable, and sustainable. Such states would see the reduction of poverty and the creation of security, social order, and wealth. Unwillingness to address structural competency deficits will only make a bad situation worse.

As noted in the introduction, the international community is gravely concerned with the emergence of failed states and the danger they pose to the international order; but at the same time, despite this concern, the international community is incapable of a trade-off between the Westphalian principle of sovereignty and a robust form of shared sovereignty within a UN-backed trusteeship framework. Limited, watered-down sovereignty arrangements, as in the case of Afghanistan, have allowed for local elites to manipulate and interfere with billions of dollars in international aid for their personal benefit while pretending to have the legitimate backing of its people.

Notes

1. Charter of the United Nations, signed on 26 June 1945 in San Francisco.
2. J.L. Holzgrefe, "The humanitarian intervention debate," in J.L. Holzgrefe and Robert O. Keohane (eds.), *Humanitarian Intervention. Ethical, legal, and Political Dilemmas,* Cambridge: Cambridge University Press, 2003 at 40.
3. Security Council Resolution 794, 3 December 1992.
4. *Ibid.*
5. Note that the *Genocide Convention,* Article 8 declares that contracting parties may legally prevent acts of genocide by calling upon "the competent organs of the United Nations to take such action...as they consider appropriate". Arguably, this does not establish a right of unauthorised humanitarian intervention. It is a topic of great debate whether the source of international law and its conventions permit unauthorised humanitarian interventions. See, *Convention on the Prevention and Punishment of the Crime of Genocide,* General Assembly Resolution 260 (III), 9 December 1948.
6. Michael Byers and Simon Chesterman, "Changing the rules about rules? Unilateral humanitarian intervention and the future of international law," in J.L. Holzgrefe and Robert O. Keohane (eds.), *Humanitarian Intervention. Ethical, legal, and Political Dilemmas,* Cambridge: Cambridge University Press, 2003 at 188.
7. Thomas Franck, "Interpretation and change in the law of humanitarian intervention," in J.L. Holzgrefe and Robert O. Keohane (eds.), *Humanitarian Intervention. Ethical, legal, and Political Dilemmas,* Cambridge: Cambridge University Press, 2003 at 214.
8. Allen Buchanan, "Reforming the international law of humanitarian intervention," in J.L. Holzgrefe and Robert O. Keohane (eds.), *Humanitarian Intervention. Ethical, legal, and Political Dilemmas,* Cambridge: Cambridge University Press, 2003 at 130.

9. Alexandros Yannis, "State Collapse and its Implications for Peace-Building and Reconstruction," in Jennifer Milliken (ed.), *State Failure, Collapse & Reconstruction,* Oxford: Blackwell Publishing, 2003 at 69.
10. *Ibid.* at 69–70.
11. J.L. Holzgrefe, "The humanitarian intervention debate," in J.L. Holzgrefe and Robert O. Keohane, *Humanitarian Intervention. Ethical, legal, and Political Dilem*mas, Cambridge: Cambridge University Press, 2003 at 48–49.
12. *The Responsibility to Protect* at 2.25.
13. The International Commission states that: "The degree of legitimacy accorded to intervention will usually turn on the answers to such questions as the purpose, the means, the exhaustion of other avenues of redress against grievances, the proportionality of the riposte to the initiating provocation, and the agency of authorisation. These are all questions that will recur: for present purposes the point is simply that there is a large and accumulating body of law and practice, which supports the notion that, whatever form the exercise of that responsibility may properly take, members of the broad community of states do have a responsibility to protect both their own citizens and those of other states as well", *The Responsibility to Protect* at 2.25.
14. In September 2011 Belgium's Deputy Prime Minister Steven Vanackere stated that sovereignty cannot stop intervention that aims to put an end to human rights abuse and the Italian Foreign Minister Franco Frattini expressed a similar view at the General Assembly and gave the example of Libya, suggesting that the only way to prevent a massacre of the Libyan people was to invoke the principle of the Responsibility to Protect. See, Belgium's Deputy Prime Minister Steven Vanackere address to the General Assembly," UN News, New York, 26 September 2011 and Italy's Foreign Minister Franco Frattini address to the General Assembly," UN News, New York, 26 September 2011.
15. "Responsibility to Protect Principle Must Cover All Who Need It," UN News, New York, 23 September 2011.
16. Daniel Thürer, *The 'Failed State' and International Law,* Geneva: International Review of the Red Cross, No. 836, 31 December 1999.
17. *W2I Mobilizing the Will to Intervene,* Montreal Institute for Genocide and Human Rights Studies, Concordia University (2010) at 3. Deng was appointed in 2012 as UN Special Adviser for the Prevention of Genocide. The Commission's report also notes that: "responsibility to protect resides first and foremost with the state whose people are directly affected. This fact reflects not only international law and the modern state system, also the practical realities of who is best placed to make a positive difference. The domestic authority is best placed to take action to prevent problems

from turning into potential conflicts. When problems arise the domestic authority is also best placed to understand them and to deal with them. When solutions are needed, it is the citizens of a particular state who have the greatest interest and the largest stake in the success of those solutions, in ensuring that the domestic authorities are fully accountable for their actions or inactions in addressing these problems, and in helping to ensure that past problems are not allowed to recur," See, *The Responsibility To Protect* at 2.30.

18. Lars Engberg-Pedersen et al, *Fragile States on the International Agenda*, Copenhagen: Danish Institute of International Studies, 2008 at 7.
19. UN Charter was signed on 26 June 1945.
20. Michael Reisman, "The Constitutional Crisis in the United Nations," *American Journal of International Law,* Vol. 87, No.1, 1993 at 89. Reisman borrows the term from American Jurist Oliver Wendell Holmes' argument about the United States Constitution.
21. *The Responsibility To Protect* at 3(A)
22. *W2I Mobilizing the Will to Intervene,* Montreal Institute for Genocide and Human Rights Studies, Concordia University, 2010 at 3.
23. *Ibid.*
24. Fernando R. Teson, "The liberal case for humanitarian intervention," in J.L. Holzgrefe and Robert O. Keohane (eds.), *Humanitarian Intervention. Ethical, legal, and Political Dilemmas,* Cambridge: Cambridge University Press, 2003 at 94.
25. "The nature of the act is itself good, or at least morally neutral; the agent intends the good effect and not the bad either as a means to the good or as an end itself; the good effect outweighs the bad effect in circumstances sufficiently grave to justify causing the bad effect and the agent exercises due diligence to minimize the harm." See, T. A. Cavanaugh, *Double-Effect Reasoning: Doing Good and Avoiding Evil,* Oxford: Oxford University Press, 2006 at 36.
26. Article 43 of the Hague Regulations notes that:"The authority of the legitimate power having in fact passed into the hands of the occupant, the latter shall take all the measures in his power to restore and ensure, as far as possible, public order and civil life, while respecting unless absolutely prevented, the laws in force in the country. International Committee of the Red Cross, International Humanitarian Law, available at: http://www.icrc.org/ihl.nsf/WebART/195-200053?OpenDocument.
27. See S. Chesterman, You, the People: The United Nations, Transitional Administration and State-Building, 2004 at Chapters 1–2.
28. Security Council Resolution 1386, adopted unanimously, 20 December 2011.

29. "The relevance of IHL in the context of terrorism," ICRC Resource Centre, 1 January 2011. Available at: http://www.icrc.org/eng/resources/documents/misc/terrorismihl- 210705.htm
30. *Ibid.*
31. The International Tribunal for the Prosecution of Persons Responsible for Serious Violations of International Humanitarian Law Committed in the Territory of the Former Yugoslavia since 1991, referred to as the International Criminal Tribunal for the former Yugoslavia or ICTY, is an ad hoc curt established by the UN (SC Resolution 827 adopted May 25, 1993) to prosecute perpetrators of serious crimes and breaches of the Geneva Conventions, genocide, war crimes committed during the wars in the former Yugoslavia. SC called upon the Tribunal to finish its work by 31 December 2014 and transfer of its responsibilities to the International Residual Mechanism for Criminal Tribunals. The Tribunal aims to complete all appeals by 2015.
32. Prosecutor v. Tadic, Appeal on Jurisdiction, Case IT-94-1-AR72 (Oct. 2, 1995), 35 I.L.M. 32, 54, para. 70, 1996.

    Also in the June 27, 1983 International Court of Justice judgment in the Nicaragua v. United States of America, the Court confirmed that Common Article 3 was applicable to the Contras who were engaged in conflict of "not of an international character".
33. Derek Jinks, "The Temporal Scope of Application of International Humanitarian Law in Contemporary Conflicts," Background Paper prepared for the Informal High-Level Expert Meeting on the Reaffirmation and Development of International Humanitarian Law, Cambridge, 27–29 January 2003.
34. "The relevance of IHL in the context of terrorism," ICRC Resource Centre, 1 January 2011. Available at:

    http://www.icrc.org/eng/resources/documents/misc/terrorism-ihl-210705.htm
35. Protocol Additional to the Geneva Conventions of 12 August 1949, and relating to the Protection of Victims of Non-International Armed Conflicts (Protocol II), 8 June 1977. There are 3 additional amending protocols: Protocol I relating to the Protection of Victims of International Armed Conflicts, Protocol II relating to the Protection of Victims of Non-International and Protocol III relating to the Adoption of an Additional Distinctive Emblem (for a humanitarian relief agency).
36. Afghanistan as a party to the International Criminal Court has the responsibility to investigate and prosecute international crimes and if unable or unwilling, the Court can exercise its jurisdiction.
37. Third Geneva Convention, Convention (III) relative to the Treatment of Prisoners of War. Geneva, 12 August 1949.

38. "The relevance of IHL in the context of terrorism," ICRC Resource Centre, 1 January 2011. Available at:

    http://www.icrc.org/eng/resources/documents/misc/terrorism-ihl-210705.htm
39. According to Roger O'Keefe, universal jurisdiction can be defined as: "prescriptive jurisdiction over offences committed abroad by persons who, at the time of commission, are non-resident aliens, where such offences are not deemed to constitute threats to the fundamental interests of the prescribing state or, in appropriate cases, to give rise to effects within its territory". See Roger O'Keefe, "Universal Jurisdiction, Clarifying the Basic Concept," *Journal of International Criminal Law,* Vol. 2, No. 3, 2004 at 745.
40. Secretary-General of the United Nations, *The scope and application of the principle* of universal jurisdiction—Report of the Secretary-General prepared on the basis of *comments and observations of Governments,* UNGAOR, 65th Session, UN Doc A/65/181, 29 July 2010 at para 19.
41. Convention relating to the Status of Refugees, 189 U.N.T.S. 150, entered into force April 22, 1954, art. 1F.
42. Universal Jurisdiction in Europe: The State of the Art, Human Rights Watch report, Volume 18, No. 5(D), June 2006.
43. The Hague District Court, October 14, 2005, AV 1489 and AV 1163, Gravenhage, 09/751005-04; official

    English translation of the judgments of both cases are available online at:

    http://zoeken.rechtspraak.nl/zoeken/dtluitspraak.asp?searchtype=ljn&ljn=AV1163&u_ljn=AV1163
44. "The Truth About Criminal Jurisdiction Over U.S. Troops in Afghanistan: Questions for Secretary of State Kerry, the Loya Jirga...and National Public Radio," Chris Jenks, Opinio Juris. Available at:

    http://opiniojuris.org/2013/10/21/guest-post-truth-criminal-jurisdiction-u-s-troopsafghanistan- questions-secretary-state-kerry-loya-jirga-national-public-radio/
45. International Court of Justice, Arrest Warrant of 11 APRIL 2000, (CONGO v. BELGIUM), Judgment, 14 February 2002 available at: http://www.world-courts.com/icj/ eng/decisions/2002.02.14_arrest_warrant.htm
46. As of 1 May 2013, 122 states will be party to the statute.
47. Text of the Rome Statute circulated as document A/CONF.183/9 of 17 July 1998 and corrected by process-verbaux of 10 November 1998, 12 July 1999, 30 November 1999, 8 May 2000, 17 January 2001 and 16 January 2002. The Statute entered into force on 1 July 2002
48. The International Controversy Court: Why its selective justice is failing Africa and the world, Sreeram Chaulia, RT online. Available at: http://rt.com/op-edge/africainternational- controversy-court-183/

49. Nele Matz, "Civilisation and the Mandate System under the League of Nations as Origin of Trusteeship," *Yearbook of United Nations Law,* Vol. 9, 2005 at 90.
50. *Ibid.* at 91–2.
51. UN Charter, Article 75.
52. United Nations Transcript of Press Conference by Secretary General Kofi Annan at the United Nation Headquarters, 8 September 2003.
53. UN Charter, Article 78.
54. UN Charter, Chapter I: Purposes and Principles, Article 2.1: "The Organisation is based on the principle of the sovereign equality of all its Members."
55. Gerald B. Helman and Steven R. Ratner, "Saving Failed States," *Foreign Policy,* No. 89, Winter 1992/93.
56. *Ibid.*
57. Lars Engberg-Pedersen et al, *Fragile States on the International Agenda,* Copenhagen: Danish Institute of International Studies, 2008 at 15.
58. *Ibid.* at 16.
59. Lars Engberg-Pedersen et al, *Fragile Situations Background Papers,* Copenhagen: Danish Institute for International Studies, 2008 at 15-16.
60. *Ibid.* at 16.
61. Michael Ignatieff, "State failure and nation-building," in J.L. Holzgrefe and Robert O. Keohane (eds.), *Humanitarian Intervention.* Ethical, legal, and Political Dilemmas, Cambridge: Cambridge University Press, 2003 at 320.
62. *The Responsibility To Protect* at 5.26.
63. *Ibid.*
64. The United Nations Transition Assistance Group (UNTAG), peacekeeping mandate from April 1989 to March 1990 in Namibia to monitor the peace process and elections there.
65. *Ibid.*
66. Nele Matz, "Civilisation and the Mandate System under the League of Nations as Origin of Trusteeship," *Yearbook of United Nations Law,* Vol. 9, 2005 at 48.
67. Gerald B. Helman and Steven R. Ratner, "Saving Failed States," *Foreign Policy,* No. 89, Winter 1992/93 at 12.
68. *Ibid.* at 3–21.
69. Ruth Gordon, "Saving Failed States: Sometimes A Neocolonialist Notion," *American University Journal of International Law and Policy,* Vol. 12, No.6, 1997 at 923.

70. Stephen D. Krasner, "Sharing Sovereignty: New Institutions for Collapsed and Failing States," International Security, Vol. 29, No. 2, Fall 2004 at 86 and 106.
71. *Ibid.* at 85–120.
72. James D. Fearon and David D. Laitin, "Neotrusteeship and the Problem of Weak States," *International Security,* Vol. 28, No.4, 2004 at 5, 36–43.
73. Stephen D. Krasner, "Sharing Sovereignty: New Institutions for Collapsed and Failing States," *International Security,* Vol. 29, No. 2, Fall 2004 at 108.
74. James D. Fearon and David D. Laitin, "Neotrusteeship and the Problem of Weak States," *International Security,* Vol. 28, No.4, 2004 at 36–7.
75. Richard Caplan, *A New Trusteeship? The International Administration of War-torn Territories:* Adelphi Paper No. 341, Oxford: Oxford University Press, 2002 at 8–9, 50–51.
76. Stephen D. Krasner, "Sharing Sovereignty: New Institutions for Collapsed and Failing States," *International Security,* Vol. 29, No. 2, Fall 2004 at 115.

Chapter 4

Application of Domestic Law

Afghan Human Rights Institutions

Over the years, Afghan women have experienced atrocious human rights violations. Amongst the waves of oppression, some positive developments have managed to take root, including the establishment of the Women's Grand Organisation in 1943 during the reign of Zahir Shah, which was to help educate women. In 1963, the organisation was incorporated into the Ministry of Labor and Social Affairs. However, throughout the period of the Islamic Emirate of Afghanistan (1996–2001), the Taliban forbad girls from going to school or work. During this period several violations were committed by government officials including "forced disappearance, arbitrary detentions, extrajudicial killing, summary execution, torture, mass killing through indiscriminate bombardment of residential areas, forced displacement, looting and destruction of public utilities and personal belongings.[1]

With the fall of the Taliban in 2001, the Ministry of Women's Affairs was established according to the agreements reached during the Bonn Conference. Dr Sima Samar was appointed the first Minister of Women's Affairs. From October 2004 until July 2006, Dr Massoda Jalal held the post.[2]

Many international observers of Afghanistan believe that women's status in that country has improved substantially after the defeat of the Taliban. In 2001, US Secretary of State Hillary Clinton noted improvements in the life expectancy of women, the number of girls attending school, and enrollments in universities since the fall of the Taliban.[3] Afghan officials also stress that things have improved radically. They point to statistics that show improvement in education and to women in various professions, who are engaged in civil and political society. Government officials claim that there are millions of girls who are no longer condemned to the "oppressed, isolated, hopeless existence they were subjected to during the war and even more brutally under the Taliban regime throughout the 1990s."[4]

In 2002, the Afghan Independent Human Rights Commission was enshrined pursuant to Article 58 of the Constitution of the Islamic Republic of Afghanistan and the Bonn Agreement of December 5, 2001, as the national human rights institution "dedicated to the promotion, protection and monitoring of human rights and the investigation of human rights abuses."[5] The current chairperson is Dr Sima Samar.

Under Article 58 of the Constitution, the Commission is

> [t]o monitor respect for human rights in Afghanistan as well as to foster and protect it, the state shall establish the Independent Human Rights Commission of Afghanistan. Every individual shall complain to this Commission about the violation of personal human rights. The Commission shall refer human rights violations of individuals to legal authorities and assist them in defense of their rights. Organisation and method of operation of the Commission shall be regulated by law.[6]

The Commission is mandated to protect and promote rights and freedoms enshrined in Afghanistan's Constitution with five objectives:

1. Monitoring the situation of human rights in the country
2. Promoting and protecting human rights
3. Monitoring the situation of and people's access to their fundamental human rights and freedoms
4. Investigating and verifying cases of human rights violations
5. Taking measures for the improvement and promotion of the human rights in the country.[7]

Dr Samar has noted that the human rights situation in Afghanistan remains bleak. Reasons include deteriorating security, systemic discrimination, weak judicial institutions, lack of access to healthcare, forced child marriage, inadequate housing, and the denial of women's rights to education and political participation.[8]

Dr Samar, whom I had the opportunity to meet during my visit with OneFreeWorld International in 2010, noted in her most recent report that the Commission's multiyear strategic plan faces significant institutional challenges, especially the lack of state funding towards the overall budget. The Commission is led by nine commissioners appointed by the president for five years.

As a member of the United Nations, Afghanistan is a party to the Universal Declaration of Human Rights. The terms of Article 7 of the Universal Declaration of Human Rights were incorporated under Chapter 2 of the Afghan Constitution. However, human rights protection exists on paper; for example, several domestic laws remain incompatible with international human rights norms.

The Karzai government, according to both domestic and international human rights reports, has failed to provide effective and appropriate mechanisms and remedies for victims of human rights violations. This failure is attributed to mistrust in the rule of law, corruption, and the incompetence of judicial institutions, with many people losing faith in the judicial system.[9]

The Afghanistan Independent Human Rights Commission has noted the failure of the Karzai government to implement laws to protect human rights and the weak rule of law, which contributes to a "high level of corruption and impunity."[10] There are still no women in the superior courts.

The Karzai government acceded to the Convention on the Elimination of All Forms of Discrimination Against Women on March 5, 2003. The Convention provides the legal framework protecting and promoting women's rights and is often called the international bill of rights for women. It was adopted in 1979 by the United Nations General Assembly and defines discrimination against women as

> any distinction, exclusion or restriction made on the basis of sex which has the effect or purpose of impairing or nullifying the

> recognition, enjoyment or exercise by women, irrespective of their marital status, on a basis of equality of men and women, of human rights and fundamental freedoms in the political, economic, social, cultural, civil or any other field.[11]

President Hamid Karzai assured Afghanistan's women that he believed in equal rights and a future where they would emerge from their houses and help rebuild the country. Critics of the regime, however, believe that change has affected only a small per centage of the population and bad laws as well as tribal mindsets continue to threaten the liberties and development of women. Dr Jalal (see Part I) is not as optimistic as those in the West; she believes that women's rights have failed to progress far enough and that many of the earlier gains are being eroded and will be further endangered after the international troops leave in 2014.

The Committee on the Elimination of Discrimination Against Women made several recommendations for prompt implementation in its July 10, 2013, periodic report on Afghanistan. The Committee notes with satisfaction the establishment of the Elite Women's Advisory Board to ensure women's engagement in the peace process; however, the process is being jeopardized by the domination of men. Out of the seventy members of the High Peace Council, only nine are women. The Doha process is further compromised by the "deep rooted patriarchal attitudes in the State party."[12] The Committee urged Afghanistan to "[i]ncrease women's representation in the High Peace Council and fully involve them effectively at all stages of the peace and reconciliation process, including by ensuring equal opportunities and active participation of women in the decision making processes."[13]

In its report, the Committee noted with concern that several members of parliament in the *Wolesi Jirga* (lower house of the bicameral National Assembly of Afghanistan) have attempted to weaken laws related to women rights and to repeal existing provisions in the Electoral Law, which provide that at least 25 per cent of seats in the provincial councils be reserved for women. The report noted with regret that the Afghan government has not yet adopted its National Action Plan to implement Security Council Resolution 1325 (2000).

Women's political participation is guaranteed under Afghanistan's constitution. Article 83 of the Constitution gives Afghan women 25 per cent of seats in the lower house, and Article 84 guarantees them almost 17 per cent in the upper house. The *Wolesi Jirga*, Afghanistan's supreme legislative body, has 249 elected seats out of which 68 are reserved for women legislators. In the last parliamentary elections held in September 2010, a total of 69 women won seats. Few of the women legislators have championed the plight of women, however; some observers note that the majority of women legislators elected are linked to powerful warlords and power brokers, and do not "have any agenda to change or improve legislation in favour of women and human rights."[14] According to parliamentarian Shinkai Karokhail, of the 68 women in parliament, "only five were vocal on women's issues. The majority of women in parliament vote in favour of more traditional legislation that often rules against women's rights."[15]

Western NGOs have worked intensively with Afghan female legislators to raise their awareness of the Afghan Constitution, parliamentary rules of procedure, the Universal Declaration of Human Rights, and the UN Convention on the Elimination of all Forms of Discrimination Against Women.

The participation of women in the legislature is not new to Afghanistan. In the 1970s, there were at least three women members of parliament, and a number of women are said to have helped draft Afghanistan's 1964 Constitution, which for the first time provided for the participation of women in the nation's legislative affairs. This Constitution, the third in the nation's history, assured all Afghans, including women, the right to vote, to become members of parliament, and to take part in political decision making. For the first time, political parties were allowed to operate publicly and not secretly, as in the past. This was also the first time that women were allowed into administrative and judicial positions.

Following the 1973 coup by Mohammad Daud Khan, women became more active in public life, not just in Kabul but also in other cities and town. In 1978, the establishment of the Revolutionary Association of Afghan Women was to provide political and social activism, helping create the new Afghanistan republic.[16]

The communist People's Democratic Party of Afghanistan, which overthrew Daud in 1978, initiated a wide range of radical reforms as soon as it took over. It promoted state atheism, forced men to shave their beards, prohibited women from wearing burqas, demanded the closure of mosques, and carried out socialist land reforms. The government also issued decrees that made education for girls as well as boys compulsory, abolished bride price (which was and still is a common practice), and changed the minimum legal age of marriage for girls to sixteen. The revolutionary zeal of the Communists, instead of transforming Afghan society, triggered a massive backlash and eventually led to the Soviet invasion and years of warfare.

On August 1, 2009, the Afghan government adopted the Elimination of Violence Against Women Law to eradicate all forms of abuse; however, the principles of Sharia were also to be enforced. The UN Assistance Mission in Afghanistan noted in a December 8, 2013, article that that "Afghan authorities registered more reports of violence against women under the Law on the Elimination of Violence against Women (EVAW law) over the past year, but prosecutions and convictions under the law remained low."[17]

The article also noted that many of the cases of violence against women are being mediated by informal dispute resolution mechanisms (*jirgas* and *shuras*) which "often fail[] to protect women from further violence by not applying criminal sanctions and legal protections for women."[18]

Shiite Personal Status Law

In February 2009, President Karzai approved the Shiite Personal Status Law, subjecting Shiite women to traditional religious controls. The Personal Status Law was introduced to provide legal status to the six million Shiite. The Shiite has long been a discriminated minority in Afghanistan, and many Shia leaders argued that the new law preserves the distinctions which are inherent between the Shia and Sunni Muslim religions of Afghanistan. The most controversial aspect of the new legislation was Article 132, which codifies marital rape by requiring women to sexually submit to their husband's demands; they are expected to have intercourse with their husbands at least once every four days and can be denied food if they refuse.[19] The law denied women the right to a divorce. They were not allowed to leave their homes or to receive an education without their husbands' permission. Many Western governments and leading human rights campaigners condemned the proposed legislation as reminiscent of the Taliban era. The legislation was negotiated by senior officials of the Karzai government and Shia members of parliament, and was quickly passed into law without much debate.

President Barack Obama called the law abhorrent: "[T]here are certain basic principles that all nations should uphold, and respect for women and respect for their freedom and integrity is an important principle."[20] Navi Pillay, the UN high commissioner for human rights, stated that the law represented

> a huge step in the wrong direction...For a new law in 2009 to target women in this way is extraordinary, reprehensible and reminiscent of the decrees made by the Taliban regime in Afghanistan in the 1990s...This is another clear indication that the human rights situation in Afghanistan is getting worse, not better.[21]

President Karzai tried to be dismissive of the legislation's critics and pointed out that the final version of the law did not ban a woman from leaving her house. Most legal scholars still argue that the current law, even with a slight amendment, contravenes the Constitution's principle of equal protection and violates some of the most basic of human rights.

Enforcement of Gender Laws

Rape is not defined in the national criminal or civil legislation in Afghanistan. Under the Afghanistan Penal Code, rape is termed *zina* (adultery), and both the victim and the perpetrators, as associates in the crime, are punished. Many young girls, having been prosecuted after being raped, find themselves in jail. Some come from forced marriages or are the victims of domestic violence. In March 2012, Human Rights Watch released a report, "'I Had to Run Away': Women and Girls Imprisoned for 'Moral Crimes' in Afghanistan," which includes fifty-eight interviews with women and girls accused of "moral crimes." The report notes the shocking reality that years after the overthrow of the Taliban, "women and girls are still imprisoned for running away from domestic violence or forced marriage...No one should be locked up for fleeing a dangerous situation even if it's at home."[22] The Human Rights report called on the government to release the proximate four hundred women and girls who were jailed for committing moral crimes.

UN special rapporteur on violence against women, Rashida Manjoo, has called for the repeal of Afghanistan's moral crimes laws and the repeal of the *zina*. These laws discriminate against women and girls, and lead to their imprisonment and cruel, inhuman, and degrading punishments.

Article 22 of the Afghan Constitution guarantees the right to nondiscrimination and the equality of all citizens; however, there is no explicit prohibition of discrimination based on sex. In many cases, the police and the prosecutors continue to refer cases related to violence against women to informal justice mechanisms (*jirgas* and *shuras*) for resolution, despite the fact that "many of these cases should be formally prosecuted and that decisions of informal justice mechanisms are discriminatory against women and undermine the implementation of existing legislation."[23]

The Elimination of Violence against Women Law was approved by presidential decree in 2009. This law makes violence against women a criminal offense but has been judged by many human rights experts as having had little practical impact on the legal status of women in Afghanistan. The government also created the Ministry of Women's Affairs. According to a joint

United Nations and Afghanistan Independent Human Rights Commission report, police and courts often fail to address sexual violence against women and incidents of domestic abuse.[24] Tribal law still dictates the norms in many rural regions, and many women still struggle for their rights.

Notes

1. Afghanistan Independent Human Rights Commission, 1389–1392 (2010–2013) Strategic Plan and Action Plan.
2. For more information available at Ministry of Women's Affairs at: http://mowa.gov.af/ en/page/1332.
3. Remarks by Hillary Rodham Clinton, Secretary of State, Benjamin Franklin Room, Washington, DC, 21 March 2012.
4. Remarks by Afghan Foreign Minister, Rassoul, Benjamin Franklin Room, Washington, DC, 21 March 2012.
5. National Human Rights Institutions and Peace Agreements: Establishing National Institutions in Divided Societies, International Council of Human Rights Policy, 2006.
6. Afghanistan Independent Human Rights Commission, 1389–1392 (2010–2013) Strategic Plan and Action Plan.
7. Afghanistan Independent Human Rights Commission, 1389–1392 (2010–2013) Strategic Plan and Action Plan, March 2010.
8. *Ibid.*
9. *Ibid.*
10. *Ibid.*
11. The Committee on the Elimination of Discrimination against Women (CEDAW) is the body of independent experts that monitors implementation of the Convention on the Elimination of All Forms of Discrimination against Women. CEDAW Committee consists of 23 experts on women's rights from around the world.
12. The Committee on the Convention on the Elimination of All Forms of Discrimination Against Women adopted the combined initial and second periodic report on Afghanistan (CEDAW/C/AFG/1–2) at its 1132nd and 1133rd meetings at its fifty-fifth session, 8–26 July 2013.
13. *Ibid.*
14. Afghan Women at the Crossroads, by Orzala Ashraf Nemat, 2011, The Century Foundation.
15. "Afghanistan's women lawmakers speak out as conditions worsen," by Clancy Chassey for the *Guardian*, 26 November 2008.
16. Orzala Ashraf Nemat, Afghan Women at the Crossroads, The Century Foundation, 2011.
17. "Mixed Results on Implantation of the EVAW Law over Pat Year," UNAMA, 8 December 2013.
18. *Ibid.*
19. Jerome Starkey, "Afghan leader accused of bid to 'legalise rape,'" The Independent (London), 31 March 2009.

20. Afghan and NATO, White House Blog, 4 April 2009. Available at: http://www.whitehouse.gov/blog/09/04/04/Afghanistan-and-NATO
21. http://seu-feminist.blogspot.com/2009_04_01_archive.html
22. "Afghanistan: Hundreds of Women, Girls Jailed for 'Moral Crimes'," Human Rights Watch, 28 March 2012. Available at: http://www.hrw.org/news/2012/03/28/afghanistanhundreds- women-girls-jailed-moral-crimes.
23. The Committee on the Convention on the Elimination of All Forms of Discrimination against Women adopted the combined initial and second periodic report on Afghanistan (CEDAW/C/AFG/1-2) at its 1132nd and 1133rd meetings at its fifty-fifth session, 8–26 July 2013.
24. Amnesty International Annual Report 2012.

Chapter 5

Terrorist Threats

Terrorism and International Law

No binding international treaties or protocols provide a definition of terrorism, which presents some legal challenges. Many states adopted domestic anti-terrorism legislation following the 9/11 attacks but clearly, following the unprecedented violence, the formulation of an international convention on terrorism and its prohibition was called for. Nonetheless, the lack of a definition in international law has not prevented the UN General Assembly and Security Council from making pronouncements on terrorism in various resolutions. In addition, several conventions and treaties do use the term "terrorism." Adding to the confusion of having no common definition of terrorism and its shifting meaning post-9/11 have been the various procedures to implement counterterrorism measures at the international level, leading to tension between establishing security and guaranteeing people's rights.[1]

The Security Council, under Chapter VII of the UN Charter, may impose various sanctions in order to maintain or restore international peace and security, and can authorize military action. On October 15, 1999, the Security

Council adopted Resolution 1267 imposing sanctions on regimes found to support terrorism, including sanctions on the Taliban regime in Afghanistan.[2] Subsequent resolutions have also been strengthened and adopted under Chapter VII and require all member states to take the following measures in connection with any individual or entity associated with Al Qaeda, as designated by the Committee:

- freeze without delay the funds and other financial assets or economic resources of designated individuals and entities [assets freeze],
- prevent the entry into or transit through their territories by designated individuals [travel ban], and
- prevent the direct or indirect supply, sale and transfer from their territories or by their nationals outside their territories, or using their flag vessels or aircraft, of arms and related materiel of all types, spare parts, and technical advice, assistance, or training related to military activities, to designated individuals and entities [arms embargo].[3]

Following the horrific terrorist attacks in New York and Washington, in Resolution 1368 (2001) the Security Council took the unprecedented step of determining that terrorism constitutes a threat to international peace and security. The resolution was adopted unanimously the following day and called on all states to bring the perpetrators to justice and for the Council to take

> all necessary steps to respond to the attacks of 11 September and to combat all forms of terrorism in accordance with its Charter responsibilities...the Council called on all States to work together urgently to bring to justice the perpetrators, organizers and sponsors of those terrorist attacks and stressed that those responsible for aiding, supporting or harbouring them would be held accountable. Also by the text, the Council held that any act of international terrorism was a threat to international peace and security. It also called on the international community to redouble its efforts to prevent and suppress terrorist acts, including by increased cooperation and full implementation of the relevant international antiterrorist conventions and Council resolutions.[4]

A UN press release coming on the heels of the resolution echoed the statement made by US President George W. Bush that "no distinction would be made between those who committed those acts and those who harboured the criminals."[5]

The Security Council's subsequent resolution (Resolution 1373) of September 28 created an international obligation to adopt specific measures to combat terrorism and called on states to take other steps to prevent and suppress terrorist acts. The resolution reaffirmed "the inherent right of individual or collective self-defence as recognised by the Charter of the United Nations as reiterated in resolution 1368 (2001), the need to combat by all means, in accordance with the Charter of the United Nations, threats to international peace and security caused by terrorist acts."[6]

The resolution also commented that the international community was increasingly concerned "by the increase, in various regions of the world, of acts of terrorism motivated by intolerance or extremism,"[7] and called on states to "work together urgently to prevent and suppress terrorist acts, including through increased cooperation and full implementation of the relevant international conventions relating to terrorism."[8] Resolution 1373 was a watershed in the international implementation of measures to combat terrorism and included the screening of asylum seekers before granting refugee status and the criminalisation under domestic law of the provision of funds to terrorist organisations. It is worth noting that according to the resolution, all states shall

(a) Prevent and suppress the financing of terrorist acts;

(b) Criminalize the wilful provision or collection, by any means, directly or indirectly, of funds by their nationals or in their territories with the intention that the funds should be used, or in the knowledge that they are to be used, in order to carry out terrorist acts;

(c) Freeze without delay funds and other financial assets or economic resources of persons who commit, or attempt to commit, terrorist acts or participate in or facilitate the commission of terrorist acts; of entities owned or controlled directly or indirectly by such persons; and of persons and entities acting on behalf of, or at the direction of such persons and entities, including funds derived or generated from property owned or controlled directly or indirectly by such persons and associated persons and entities;

(d) Prohibit their nationals or any persons and entities within their territories from making any funds, financial assets or economic resources or financial or other related services available, directly or indirectly, for the benefit of persons who commit or attempt to commit or facilitate or participate in the commission of terrorist acts, of entities owned or controlled, directly or indirectly, by such persons and of persons and entities acting on behalf of or at the direction of such persons.[9]

The Security Council also decided that all states shall

(a) Refrain from providing any form of support, active or passive, to entities or persons involved in terrorist acts, including by suppressing recruitment of members of terrorist groups and eliminating the supply of weapons to terrorists;

(b) Take the necessary steps to prevent the commission of terrorist acts, including by provision of early warning to other States by exchange of information;

(c) Deny safe haven to those who finance, plan, support, or commit terrorist acts, or provide safe havens;

(d) Prevent those who finance, plan, facilitate or commit terrorist acts from using their respective territories for those purposes against other States or their citizens;

(e) Ensure that any person who participates in the financing, planning, preparation or perpetration of terrorist acts or in supporting terrorist acts is brought to justice and ensure that, in addition to any other measures against them, such terrorist acts are established as serious criminal offences in domestic laws and regulations and that the punishment duly reflects the seriousness of such terrorist acts;

(f) Afford one another the greatest measure of assistance in connection with criminal investigations or criminal proceedings relating to the financing or support of terrorist acts, including assistance in obtaining evidence in their possession necessary for the proceedings;

(g) Prevent the movement of terrorists or terrorist groups by effective border controls and controls on issuance of identity papers and travel documents, and through measures for preventing counterfeiting, forgery or fraudulent use of identity papers and travel documents.[10]

Council called upon all states to

(a) Find ways of intensifying and accelerating the exchange of operational information, especially regarding actions or movements of terrorist persons or networks; forged or falsified travel documents; traffic in arms, explosives or sensitive materials; use of communications technologies by terrorist groups; and the threat posed by the possession of weapons of mass destruction by terrorist groups;

(b) Exchange information in accordance with international and domestic law and cooperate on administrative and judicial matters to prevent the commission of terrorist acts;

(c) Cooperate, particularly through bilateral and multilateral arrangements and agreements, to prevent and suppress terrorist attacks and take action against perpetrators of such acts;

(d) Become parties as soon as possible to the relevant international conventions and protocols relating to terrorism, including the International Convention for the Suppression of the Financing of Terrorism of 9 December 1999;

(e) Increase cooperation and fully implement the relevant international conventions and protocols relating to terrorism and Security Council resolutions 1269 (1999) and 1368 (2001);

(f) Take appropriate measures in conformity with the relevant provisions of national and international law, including international standards of human rights, before granting refugee status,for the purpose of ensuring that the asylum-seeker has not planned, facilitated or participated in the commission of terrorist acts;

(g) Ensure, in conformity with international law, that refugee status is not abused by the perpetrators, organizers or facilitators of terrorist acts, and that claims of political motivation are not recognised as grounds for refusing requests for the extradition of alleged terrorists.

> Finally, the Security Council also noted with concern the close connection between international terrorism and transnational organised crime, illicit drugs, money-laundering, illegal arms-trafficking, and illegal movement of nuclear, chemical, biological and other potentially deadly materials, and in this regard emphasizes the need to enhance coordination of efforts on national, subregional, regional and international levels in order to strengthen a global response to this serious challenge and threat to international security.[11]

The implementation of counterterrorism measures as defined by the Security Council is not just a matter of national policy; an international obligation has been created under Chapter VII of the Charter for states to take measures and thus under international law to implement specific measures as set out in Resolution 1373. A counterterrorism committee was established following Resolution 1373 to monitor the implementation of the resolution and to review states' reports.

The Security Council has said that terrorism is an act that constitutes "a threat to international peace and security." In this sense, the measures specified in Resolution 1373 and the other counterterrorist measures that states are requested to implement refer only to the most serious crimes under international law. This characteristic (the gravity of the act) has been implemented in several domestic legislations. Many nations today would argue that counterterrorism measures must be compatible with other international obligations, particularly the need to respect international human rights and humanitarian law, as outlined in international treaty obligations.

Targeting Terrorist

The legality of the war on terrorism and the drone attacks targeting terrorists is a highly controversial issue in international law and requires further analysis in international humanitarian law. The targeting of terrorists is complicated by the reality that civilians have also become victims from direct drone attacks and aerial bombardments. For example, the United States has successfully targeted Al Qaeda and

Taliban leaders, who have hidden in tribal areas of Pakistan, but several civilians have also been killed.

The US administration has acknowledged the need for new policy guidelines related to targeted killings but has at the same time justified targeted killing using drones or cruise missiles as part a comprehensive counterterrorism strategy. A special UN report notes that targeted killing is not a term distinctly defined under international law.[12] The White House has stated that there is proper oversight of drone strikes; they are carried out according to the domestic laws that Congress approved following the 9/11 attacks, which included the use of all necessary and appropriate force to pursue those responsible for the attacks. It has been a difficult balancing act for President Obama, who was given broad powers to act domestically and internationally against any perceived threat while adhering to human rights and international law.

The United States argue that they are still in a state of armed conflict with "non-state actors," who operate in loose transnational networks; the States, therefore, have the right to self-defense, a major principal of national security. Certainly, the targeted killing by a US Navy SEAL raid on bin Laden was not condemned by the international community and was seen by some as international justification for US actions. Bin Laden was hiding in Abbotabad, Pakistan, when the Al Qaeda leader was killed on May 2, 2011.

Questions of state sovereignty are of concern in such cases. Pakistan protested against the United States' unilateral action on their soil, but given credible reports that many members of Pakistan's Inter-Services Intelligence (ISI) are supporters or members of Al Qaeda, most observers would agree that it was a wise move by the US government to attack preemptively without any prior consent from the Pakistan government.

Philip Alston, former UN special rapporteur on extrajudicial, summary, or arbitrary executions, has voiced the concern of other critics: "If other states were to claim the broad-based authority that the United States does— to kill people anywhere, anytime—the result would be chaos."[13]

According to a recent study, President Obama has authorised nearly four times as many strikes in Pakistan as President Bush during his two terms as president. The report also notes that the majority of the attacks are managed by the Central Intelligence Agency with support from the Defense Department. As of 2013, President Obama has shifted the responsibility more to the Defense Department.

The raids are very unpopular with local tribal leaders on the Afghanistan-Pakistan border, especially raids carried out in the middle of the night that result in civilian casualties. Afghan and Pakistani governments and parliaments have called for an end to the drone attacks but their motives are unclear. Human rights groups have widely condemned the practice of targeted killings as well as the program's accountability and transparency.

The insurgency group linked to the Taliban causes the vast majority of civilian casualties. Both the First Additional Protocol of June 8, 1977, to the 1949 Geneva Conventions[14] and the Rome Statute provide clarity on attacks against civilians. According to the UN Assistance Mission in Afghanistan 2013 report, there was a 23 per cent rise in the number of civilian casualties in 2013 compared to 2012. The report documents "1,319 civilian deaths and 2,533 injuries in the first half of 2013, marking increases of 14 per cent in deaths and 28 per cent in injuries over the same period in 2012."[15] This rise in deaths and injuries during the critical transitional phase prior to the 2014 withdrawal is troubling given that 74 per cent of all civil casualties were due to actions taken by antigovernment elements.[16]

Afghan-Pakistan Taliban Nexus

Cross border skirmishes have been ongoing for many decades in the region of the poorly marked Durand Line of Afghanistan and Pakistan. Afghanistan has always refused to recognize the Durand Line as its international border. The ever-increasing militant insurgency of the tribal rebellion in the Swat district has produced serious instability in both Afghanistan and Pakistan. The situation in the nuclear-state Pakistan is just as precarious, with factionalised elites and tribal unrest. Afghanistan's and Pakistan's lack of control over many parts of their own territory further complicates this volatile mix.[17] Much of this fighting is tribal, and the various allegiances cross seemingly invisible international boundaries.

Pakistan's military has been fighting domestic insurgencies since the country's tumultuous birth just over a half century ago. In the past two years, under intense pressure from the United States, Pakistan has fought a series of offensive campaigns against a mounting Taliban presence in the northwestern regions of the country. The army has been largely ineffective against the relentless Taliban militia, which poses a serious threat to both Afghanistan and Pakistan. Some commentators have argued that this problem is a monster of Pakistan's own creation.[18]

Analysts note that Pakistani security agencies are failing to provide security against these militants, while 2006 leaked report by the British Defense Ministry charged that "indirectly Pakistan (through the ISI) has been supporting terrorism and extremism—whether in London on 7/7 [the July 2005 attacks on London's transit system], or in Afghanistan, or Iraq."[19] US Defense Secretary Robert Gates has accused Pakistan, which is a recipient of substantial US funding, of playing both sides and suggests the Pakistan ISI "maintains links with groups like the Afghan Taliban as a 'strategic hedge' to help Islamabad gain influence in Kabul once U.S. troops exit the region."[20] Although the Pakistani government has denied the allegations, they were reiterated by US Chairman of the Joint Chiefs of Staff Admiral Mike Mullen during a visit to Pakistan in April 2011, who pointed to ISI's links to the Haqqani network.[21]

A June 2010 report by the Carr Center for Human Rights Policy at the Kennedy School of Government in Harvard University notes that according to Taliban commanders, the ISI "orchestrates, sustains and strongly influences the movement. They say it gives sanctuary to both Taliban and Haqqani groups, and provides huge support in terms of training, funding, munitions, and supplies. In their words, this is 'as clear as the sun in the sky'"[22] According to the US Congressional Research Service report summary,

> [m]any analysts believe that Pakistan's intelligence services know the whereabouts of...Afghan Taliban leadership elements and

likely even maintain active contacts with them at some level as part of a hedge strategy in the region. Some reports indicate that elements of Pakistan's major intelligence agency and military forces aid the Taliban.[23]

Anita Demkiv's article in the Journal of Global Change and Governance comments that Pakistan

> is one of the least stable countries possessing nuclear weapons...the Federally Administered Tribal Areas (FATA) harbours exiled Taliban leaders and al Qaeda's leadership; and there is an ongoing radicalisation throughout the country—not limited to the FATA. As seen in the December 2008 attacks on Mumbai, the security of countries near and far could be gravely affected by Pakistan's inability to reign in terrorist elements.[24]

The genesis of Pakistan's present crisis has its roots in the 1970s, when the country became a strategic ally in the cold war crusade being led by the United States against Communism. In launching an anti-Soviet jihad, Pakistan and its Western supporters strengthened militant Islamist forces and encouraged the growth of a group of radical, drug-smuggling, Kalashnikovwielding warlord elites.[25]

The US-led NATO coalition that spearheaded the UN-sanctioned invasion of Afghanistan in October 2001 sought the help of Pakistan from the very outset of this undertaking. The expectation was that Pakistan would help the coalition in rooting out insurgents as well as ensuring that the militants did not find safe havens within the country.[26] Pakistan was always widely rumored to be the hiding place of Osama bin Laden, and it was not until Operation Neptune Spear was carried out by the US Naval Special Warfare Development Group in May 2, 2011, that that suspicion was confirmed. Pakistan came under intense international scrutiny after the raid; bin Laden's compound was near Pakistan Military Academy in Abbottabad.

Pakistan's government maintains that it is serious in its efforts to tackle the Taliban; however, many doubts remain over the army's willingness to fight. There are reports that the Pakistan army sees the Taliban as a useful counterweight to the perceived growing influence in Central Asia of perennial rival India. At the moment, it seems implausible that Pakistan could successfully defeat the militants—nor has the international community been assured that the current president, Mamnoon Hussain Zardari, and prime minister, Nawaz Sharif, have the political will to tackle the crisis.

Afghan-Pakistan Insurgency

The insurgents, such as the North Waziristan–based Haqqani Network and the Pakistani Taliban (also known as the Tehrik-e-Taliban and Lashkar-e-Jhangvi) "systematically work to undermine the Government of Pakistan."[27]

According to a July 18, 2013, United States House Committee on Foreign Affairs, Subcommittee on Terrorism report, Al Qaeda is defined as a "global international terrorist network, with a general command in Afghanistan and Pakistan and affiliates in several countries. Together, they form a robust network that, despite setbacks, contests for territory abroad and still poses a threat to U.S. interests both overseas and at home."[28]

The Haqqani Network on the border of Afghanistan and Pakistan has strong links to Al Qaeda. Pakistan provides safe havens from which to launch direct attacks on NATO forces. The Haqqani Network "has long served as a local enabler of al Qaeda and its global jihad."[29]

In March 2012, Commander General John R. Allen stated to the US House Armed Services Committee that

> if we don't see Pakistani action to address the safe havens, then ultimately we're going to have to thicken the defences of the Afghan people to provide as much friction as possible to protect the strategic centre of gravity, which is Kabul and the security zone around Kabul. And we anticipate that that's probably going to have to become an outcome.

US airstrikes on November 26, 2011, killed twenty-four Pakistani troops, which resulted in a deterioration of relations, with Pakistan closing the NATO supply route to Afghanistan for nearly a year. Pakistan has yet to accept the conclusions of the US investigation and has made logistics cooperation between NATO forces and those of Pakistan troublesome. The ill feelings between the United States and

Pakistan are further challenged by the withdrawal of troops from Afghanistan in 2014. If Pakistan does not cooperate and relations do not improve, this antipathy will have long term consequences for Afghanistan's security and stability. NATO forces are working with the Afghan National Army to build capacity and to take a more active role in combat operations; however, the Afghan National Army is still greatly dependent on NATO.

A UN report notes that the Taliban is responsible for the vast majority of civilian deaths, "more than three-fourths (76 per cent) of civilian deaths in Afghanistan over the past year have been caused by the Taliban (12 per cent of civilian deaths can be traced to Coalition forces)."[30]

The Taliban's supreme leader, Mullah Omar, has ordered his forces "to kill or capture any civilians, including Afghan women, who cooperate with Coalition forces. Omar's latest directive contradicts his marching orders from just one year ago, when he told his Taliban commanders to refrain from harming civilians working with the Coalition."[31]

The Taliban still want to impose an Islamic emirate on the Afghan population and according to a NATO Parliamentary Assembly report, the Taliban "statements show that they believe the Islamic Emirate of Afghanistan remains a reality, even if they do not control the cities."[32]

Notes

1. Counter-terrorism measures have strengthened cooperation and intelligence-sharing between police departments and security intelligence services and the adoption of new legislation to deal with the financing of terrorist activity. See examples of UN Security Council Resolution 1373 (2001) of 28 September 2001, S/RES/1373 (2001) and UN Security Resolution 1267/1999 of 15 October 1999.
2. The sanctions regime was first established by resolution 1267 (1999) on 15 October 1999 and has been modified and strengthened by subsequent resolutions, including resolutions 1333 (2000), 1390 (2002), 1455 (2003), 1526 (2004), 1617 (2005), 1735 (2006), 1822 (2008), 1904 (2009), 1989 (2011) and resolution 2083 (2012) so that the sanctions measures now apply to designated individuals and entities associated with Al-Qaida, wherever located. The names of the targeted individuals and entities are placed on the Al-Qaida Sanctions List.

3. The sanctions regime was first established by resolution 1267 (1999) on 15 October 1999 and has been modified and strengthened by subsequent resolutions, including resolutions 1333 (2000), 1390 (2002), 1455 (2003), 1526 (2004), 1617 (2005), 1735 (2006), 1822 (2008), 1904 (2009), 1989 (2011) and resolution 2083 (2012) so that the sanctions measures now apply to designated individuals and entities associated with Al-Qaida, wherever located. The names of the targeted individuals and entities are placed on the Al-Qaida Sanctions List. Narrative summaries of reasons for listing of the individuals, groups, undertakings and entities included in the Al-Qaida Sanctions List can be found at the following URL: /sc/committees/1267/narrative.shtml and at: http://www.un.org/sc/committees/1267/
4. Security Council Condemns, 'In Strongest Terms', Terrorist Attack on United States, Unanimously Adopting Resolution 1368 (2001), Council Calls on All States to Bring Perpetrators to Justice, UN News, 12 September 2001. Available at: http://www. un.org/News/Press/docs/2001/SC7143.doc.htm
5. *Ibid.*
6. Security Council adopted Resolution 1373 (2001) at its 4385th meeting, on 28 September 2001.
7. *Ibid.*
8. *Ibid.*
9. Security Council Unanimously Adopted Wide-Ranging Anti-Terrorism Resolution, Calls for Suppressing Financing, Improving International Cooperation, Resolution 1373 (2001) Also Creates Committee to Monitor Implementation, UN News, 28 September 2001.
10. *Ibid.*
11. *Ibid.*
12. According to a UN special report on the subject, targeted killings are premeditated acts of lethal force employed by states in times of peace or during armed conflict to eliminate specific individuals outside their custody.
13. Jonathan Masters, "Targeted Killings," Council on Foreign Relations, 23 May 2013.
14. Protocol Additional to the Geneva Conventions of 12 August 1949, and relating to the Protection of Victims of International Armed Conflicts (Protocol I), 8 June 1977. Available at: http://www.icrc.org/applic/ihl/ihl.nsf/Treaty.xsp?action=openDocument &documentId=D9E6B6264D7723C3C12563CD002D6CE4.
15. UNAMA report shows sharp rise in casualties among Afghan civilians in first half of 2013. Available at: http://unama.unmissions.org/Default.aspx?ctl=Details&tabid=12 254&mid=15756&ItemID=37114.

16. Amnesty International 2012 Report on Afghanistan. Available at: https://www.amnesty. org/en/region/afghanistan/report-2012.
17. What is Happening in Pakistan? Hilary Synnott, Survival: Global Politics and Strategy, 1468–2699, Volume 51, Issue 1, 2009 at 65.
18. Christophe Jaffrelot, A History of Pakistan and Its Origins at 270.
19. Ayshree Bajoria and Eben Kaplan, "The ISI and Terrorism: Behind the Accusations," Council on Foreign Relations, 4 May 2011.
20. *Ibid.*
21. *Ibid.*
22. Matt Waldman, "The Sun in the Sky: The relationship between Pakistan's ISI and Afghan insurgents," Crisis States Research Centre, June 2010.
23. K. Alan Kronstadt, "Pakistan-U.S. Relations," Congressional Research Service, 1 July 2009.
24. Anita Demkiv, Division of Global Affairs, Rutgers University Journal of Global Change and Governance, Volume II, Number 1, Winter/Spring 2009.
25. *Ibid.*
26. Stuart Notholt, Fields of Fire—An Atlas of Ethnic Conflict, 2008.
27. Al Qaeda, the Taliban, and other extremist groups in Afghanistan and Pakistan, Hearing before the Committee on Foreign Relations, United States Senate, 24 May 2011.
28. Thomas Joscelyn, United States House Committee on Foreign Affairs, Subcommittee on Terrorism report, July 18, 2013.
29. Brown, Vahid and Rassler, Don. Fountainhead of Jihad: The Haqqani Nexus, 1973–2012. New York: Columbia University Press, 2013 at 229.
30. Bill Roggio, "UN: Taliban Responsible for 76 per cent of Deaths in Afghanistan: The Taliban provided two high-profile instances of their deliberate targeting of civilians in the past week," The Weekly Standard, 10 August 2010.
31. Thomas Joscelyn and Bill Roggio, "Mullah Omar orders Taliban to attack civilians, Afghan women," The Long War Journal, 28 July 2010.
32. Afghanistan: Toward 2014 and Beyond, NATO Parliamentary Assembly, 5 April 2012.

Chapter 6

Enduring Strategic Partnership Agreement

The Lisbon Roadmap

In November 2010, NATO representatives and the government of Afghanistan signed the Declaration on Enduring Partnership in Lisbon and reaffirmed "its long-term commitment to a sovereign, independent, democratic, secure and stable Afghanistan that will never again be a safe haven for terrorists and terrorism, and to a better future for the Afghan people"[1]

In April 2012, in Kabul, Afghan President Hamid Karzai and US President Barack Obama agreed to a long-awaited deal on the pullout of troops in 2014. The strategic partnership agreement proposed a framework for a longterm relationship between Afghanistan and the United States after 2014. The legally binding agreement is officially known as Enduring Strategic Partnership Agreement Between the Islamic Republic of Afghanistan and the United States of America.[2] A series of commitments and statements have pledged NATO to combat terrorism and respect human rights, and to further cooperation and security assistance. The agreement—although some call it the exit strategy—was further outlined and elaborated in late May, 2012, at the Summit of NATO Heads of State in Chicago. NATO made the commitment to withdraw forces by 2014, with the Afghan National Security Forces (ANSF) taking sole responsibility for combat missions.

The Partnership Agreement will determine future military operations specified in the Bilateral Security Agreement over the course of the next ten years. Of course, these agreements will depend on the incoming government in Afghanistan. Long-term cooperation is not guaranteed and could weaken in the face of growing insurgency or political setbacks.

The US Embassy spokesman in Kabul stated that the goal is "an enduring partnership with Afghanistan that strengthens Afghan sovereignty, stability and prosperity and that contributes to our shared goal of defeating Al Qaeda and its extremist affiliates. We believe this agreement supports that goal."[3]

The ten-year Strategic Partnership Agreement includes mutual commitments in five key areas: (1) protecting and promoting shared democratic values, (2) advancing long-term security, (3) reinforcing regional security and cooperation, (4) social and economic development, and (5) strengthening Afghan institutions and governance.[4] According to the White House, the Strategic Partnership Agreement "does not commit the United States to any specific troop levels or levels of funding in the future."[5]

President Karzai also wanted the United States to make a multiyear financial commitment to the Afghan Army and police force post-2014; in a recent statement, he hoped for the United States to contribute US$2 billion a year.[6] President Karzai's performance during the negotiations has been highly criticized. He has constantly forced demands upon the United States and insisted that the United States not meddle in the upcoming elections.[7]

The Strategic Partnership Agreement designated Afghanistan a major non-NATO ally of the United States.[8] This position will facilitate the Afghanistan government to purchase US military equipment and to gain long-term defense cooperation.

The Agreement was endorsed by the *loya jirga* on November 24, 2013. Karzais' attitude, however, continues to be troubling. He has hinted that he may not sign the agreement until after the April 2014 elections and has asked for a national consensus before reaching a decision on whether to forward the agreement to parliament for final approval.[9] Critics have argued that his speech during the meeting with two thousand five hundred tribal elders of the *loya jirga* not to sign the legal framework was a strategy to influence the upcoming presidential elections.

Transition Pillars after Withdrawal

Transitioning from state failure to a functioning society is never easy and is all the more complicated when active insurgents desire to seize power. Necessary conditions for transition include the building of the Afghan National Security Forces and the Afghan National Police and well as the rule of law with a functioning judicial system. These institutions had to be built from nothing following the fall of the Taliban, and billions of dollars from mainly Western countries have been used during the transition period to adequately train and arm the Afghan forces. However, several reports point out concerning deficiencies in the Afghan National Security Forces' logistical capabilities, some of them due to a huge problem with poor literacy among the forces. The Afghan National Army Trust Fund is a special fund from donor countries, which amounted to US$700 million in 2013, with additional millions from the United States. The Law and Order Trust Fund is organised by the UN Development Program and from

> 2002–2012, donors contributed $2.75 billion to the Fund, of which the United States contributed about $1 billion. Japan's 2009 pledge to pay the expenses of the Afghan police for at least six months (about $125 million for each six month period) is implemented through the LOTF. The EU pledged $175 million for the fund from January 2011–March 2013.[10]

The United States added an additional "$2.7 billion worth of vehicles, weapons, equipment, and aircraft...during August 2011–March 2012."[11]

It is an open question whether the Taliban are emboldened by the upcoming troop withdrawal. The objective of the US-Afghan negotiations is a long-term security deal, but the hardening of positions on both sides of the talks could lead to a repetition of what happened in Iraq. There has also been tension in relations between civilian and military officials in Washington.

UN Secretary-General Ban Ki-moon's Special Representative Jan Kubiš has noted in his report to the Security Council on the UN Assistance Mission in Afghanistan that the situation in Afghanistan will require ambitious security, political and economic transformations for the next decade:

> We must resolutely continue working together to ensure a sovereign and sustainable State that will never again become a haven for international terrorism and organised crime, notably including narco-businesses. This is in everyone's interest.[12]

Mr. Kubiš highlighted the "critical importance" of holding credible presidential elections and warned that the "security challenges are real and should be proactively and realistically addressed to promote maximum inclusion and avoid any pretext for disenfranchisement or delay."[13]

Kubiš has also underscored the need for international observation efforts to help Afghanistan during the electoral process and for direct talks between the Afghan authorities and anti-government forces. He has warned of "the potential for volatility post-2014 if there is a vacuum which could encourage the spread of Al-Qaeda-linked international terrorism and criminality with implications across the region."[14]

There is much debate and apprehension over how the Afghanistan National Security Forces will operate after 2014. Some military experts believe that the small, residual force will enable the Taliban to make gains and unravel the Afghan security forces.

In 2010, the Obama administration began to make it clear that the US troops would be leaving Afghanistan by the end of 2014. The Karzai government has attempted to broker a peace deal with the Taliban before the pullout but has failed to involve women's human rights groups in the process. Despite the Taliban's brutal history of repression, Taliban representatives are participating at the Doha conference, and the Taliban has even opened a political office in Qatar. The Taliban continues to declare that the current constitution is illegitimate because it was authored by the United States and, incredibly, to claim to be the legitimate government of the country. Women have no desire to become victims of "peace" and they, as well as other groups, have criticised the Taliban's increasing political involvement.

In 2010, the Afghan Peace and Reintegration Program was launched with offers of amnesty to former Taliban fighters if they relinquished violence and respected the Afghan Constitution. In one of the last resolutions of 2013, the Security Council reaffirmed that the Afghanistan peace process "lies in the building of a stable, secure, economically sustainable state, free of terrorism and narcotics and based on the rule of law, strengthened democratic institutions, respect for the separation of powers, reinforced constitutional checks and balances and the guarantee and enforcement of citizens' rights and obligations."[15]

The Afghan parliament had approved a controversial amnesty law in 2007, which recognised the right of war crimes victims to seek justice but also banned the prosecution of Taliban fighters accused of war crimes. Many scholars and human rights activists argued that the amnesty would damage the prospects of national reconciliation.[16]

Wadir Safi, a professor of law and political science at Kabul University, notes with anger that the amnesty should not have been passed given that many of the present lawmakers are themselves alleged to have committed war crimes: "Let us say that passing this legislation was not within the powers of the lower house of parliament...This means that the representatives of the lower house shouldn't be the judges of their own deeds."[17]

Among the alleged war crimes, it is claimed that thousands of civilians were killed by both the Mujahideen resistance fighters and the Taliban, during its rule. The bill would effectively shield those accused of human rights violations.[18]

Notes

1. http://www.reuters.com/article/2012/04/22/us-afghanistan-agreementid USBRE83L07S20120422.
2. http://www.whitehouse.gov/sites/default/files/2012.06.01u.s.-afghanistan-spasigned text.pdf
3. "US, Afghanistan reach partnership deal," The Sydney Morning Herald, 23 April 2012.

4. "Fact Sheet: The U.S.-Afghanistan Strategic Partnership Agreement," The White House Press available at:

   http://www.whitehouse.gov/the-press-office/2012/05/01/fact-sheet-us-afghanistanstrategic- partnership-agreement.

5. *Ibid.*

6. Rob Taylor, "Afghanistan and U.S. agree on strategic pact text," Reuters, 22 April 2012.

   Available at: http://www.reuters.com/article/2012/04/22/us-afghanistan-agreementidUSBRE83L07S20120422.

7. Tim Craig, "Afghan elders endorse U.S. troops' presence but President Karzai still refuses to sign," Washington Post, 24 November 2013.

8. "Major Non-NATO Ally Status for Afghanistan," U.S. Department of State, 7 July 2012.

9. "Hagel voices frustration with Afghan foot-dragging," Military Times, 30 January 2014.

10. Kenneth Katzman, Afghanistan: Post-Taliban Governance, Security, and U.S. Policy, Congressional Research Service, 23 October 2013.

11. *Ibid.*

12. Afghanistan is Advancing Towards Stability as International Force Draws Down—UN Envoy, New York, 17 December 2013.

13. *Ibid.*

14. *Ibid.*

15. Security Council Resolution 2120 (2013) adopted at its 7041st meeting, 10 October 2013.

16. Ron Synovitz, "Amnesty Law Draws Criticism, Praise," Radio Free Europe, 16 March 2007.

17. *Ibid.*

18 "Afghanistan: President pressured to sign controversial amnesty bill," IRIN News, 26 February 2007.

Conclusion

The framework that has been laid out for Afghanistan following the 2014 withdrawal will greatly depend on the new administration for its successful implementation. It will be up to the new government to ensure that women's rights are protected and maintained and that the persisting insecurity and threats of violence are dealt with effectively. The current situation, which continues to be a source of great concern, presents a multitude of challenges for the new administration as well as the international community.

The approaching transition of power will be an important test for the democratic institutions of Afghanistan, and an orderly presidential election would be a bright spot in an otherwise uncertain future. The international community is intensely interested in a stable Afghanistan and an orderly transition of security responsibilities to the Afghan military forces. The last term of the Karzai government sees much left undone. Karzai's defiant tone and unwillingness to sign the Bilateral Security Agreement with the United States months before the US troops are to leave Afghanistan is making the transition even more difficult than it already is. His persistence in pursuing talks with the Taliban will ultimately lead to a weak government and a weakening of human rights, especially for women.

2014 is critical for Afghanistan, and happenings over the next few months could lead to another civil war. The international community has made a series of strategic assumptions that underpin the withdrawal; however, more than a decade after the ousting of the Taliban from power, Afghanistan is still on the verge of reverting to a failed state.

Appendix A

Excerpts: Afghanistan Law on the Elimination of Violence against Women

Sexual Abuse

Sexual Assault/Rape (article 17)

Sexual assault and rape mean sexual acts with a woman or girl that is performed against her will, with force, or pressure. It includes sexual intercourse, as well as touching that violates the chastity and honor of a woman. The Penal Code in Article 429(1) also explains that "a person who, through violence, threat or deceit, violates the chastity of another, or initiates the act" may be sentenced to up to 7 years in prison.

Sexual assault or rape is a crime when committed by anyone. It is a crime when it is committed by a stranger, or an acquaintance, a friend, relative, teacher, co-worker, doctor, or anyone who has influence and authority over the victim. Depending on the type of sexual assault committed, the perpetrator may be punished with sentences ranging from no more than 7 years to life in prison. In cases where the victim dies, the criminal may be sentenced to the death penalty.

Forcing into prostitution (article 18)

It is a crime to force a woman to sell her body or to have sex in exchange for payment or goods (for example, food, clothes, jewelry, and shelter or housing). The punishment for this crime ranges from 7 years in prison, to more than 10 years if the victim is under 18 years of age.

Recording and publishing the identity of victims (article 19)

It is a crime to record the identity of the victim of rape or forced prostitution (for example, to take a picture or use the name of the victim) and to publish or broadcast their pictures in the media, internet, or other public places which will damage their reputation or integrity.

Burning or using chemicals or poisons to injure or intimidate (article 20)

It is a crime for any person to burn a woman or spray chemicals or other harmful substances on her body causing injury, or to force a woman to eat harmful substances or inject such substances into her body.

Forcing women to burn themselves or commit suicide (article 21)

It is illegal to mistreat women in ways that push them to burn themselves, swallow poison, or commit suicide. The punishment is more severe if the woman suffers injury or disability from these actions.

Causing injury or disability (article 22)

Abuse or beating of a woman or girl which results in her injury or disability is a crime and the abuser will be punished under the criminal law, with imprisonment of 3 months to 10 years depending on the severity and impact of the injury. Beatings causing injury or disability include cutting, causing defects or handicap, loss of one of the senses, harm or paralysis of a body part.

Beating (article 23)

It is a crime to beat women or girls, even when no injury or disability results from the beating. Hitting, shoving, and slapping that do not cause bleeding or broken bones are also prohibited. Anyone who beats a woman (including the husband, an uncle, parents or, parents-in-law) may be sentenced for up to 3 month imprisonment.

It is considered an especially serious crime to use chemicals or poisons against women and girls for the purpose of spreading fear and terror in order to prevent women from accessing their rights, such as their right to education or to employment.

Emotional and Psychological Abuse Humiliation, intimidation, and harassment (articles 29-30)

Cursing, intimidating, or humiliating a woman are considered degrading acts that can be punished under the law. Intimidating a woman means using bad, abusive, or insulting words or acting in ways to frighten or threaten her, for example threatening to beat or harm the woman or her children, or threatening to fire her from a job, dismiss her from school, or refuse to give her legal or medical services unless she performs certain sexual acts. Prohibited harassment includes using words and actions that hurt a woman's reputation, body, or mental wellbeing.

Anyone who violates this part of the law may be sentenced to no less than 3 months in prison. A person who uses his position of authority to harass a woman may receive a longer sentence of at least 6 months in prison.

Selling and buying women for marriage (article 24)

It is a criminal act to sell or buy a woman for marriage or under the pretext of marriage. Any person who takes or gives money or other valuables (toyanah) or who facilitates such an exchange of a woman as if for marriage will be punished with up to 10 years in prison.

Baad (article 25)

It is a criminal act to marry or "give away" girls and women to someone as blood price. The law prohibits the trading of women and girls to resolve disputes, including those related to murder, sexual violence, or other harmful acts.

A person who gives or takes a woman for marriage in retribution for a Baad may be prosecuted and punished with up to 10 years in prison.

Any person who is involved in giving women as Baad will also be punished, including any witnesses, mediators, and the persons conducting the marriage ceremony. A marriage that results from Baad is considered invalid.

Forced marriage (article 26)

An engagement or marriage without the woman's consent is invalid. Any person who is involved in forcing a girl over 16 to become engaged or marry without her agreement may be sentenced to 2 or more years in prison.

Prohibiting woman to marry or choose a husband (article 27)

No one may deprive or prevent a woman from choosing who she would like to marry or prohibit her from marrying the person of her choice. Anyone who prohibits a woman from freely choosing her husband will be subject to short term imprisonment.

Crimes related to Marriage

Marriage before the legal age (article 28)

It is generally illegal to marry a girl who has not reached the legal age of marriage, which is 16 years of age. Under the civil code, in some situations, the father or the court may authorize the marriage of a girl who is 15 years old.

It is illegal under any circumstance to marry a girl who is under 15 (Civil Code, article 71). A marriage of a girl under 15 will be cancelled at the request of the girl. The person who marries a girl under 15 will be punished with a prison term of at least 2 years.

Isolating a woman from her family (article 31)

It is a crime to isolate a woman in the home, or from her relatives. For example, it is against the law to prevent a woman from visiting her parents or other close relatives (legal mahrams). The offender may be sentenced to a maximum of 3 months in prison.

Forcing woman to drug addiction (article 32)

No one may force or pressure a woman to take narcotic drugs, such as hashish, heroin, opium, or other drugs, that would cause her to become addicted, or dependant on the drug. The punishment for causing women to become addicted to drugs is a maximum sentence of 3 months in prison.

Deprivation of Property and Inheritance

Deprivation of inheritance (article 33)

No person may deny a woman or girl her inheritance, or her share of property from her deceased husband, father, or other relative. She must be given her legal share of the property and the person who tries to prevent her from getting her share may be sentenced to up to 3 months imprisonment.

Preventing access to personal property (article 34)

No one may prevent a woman from having or getting personal property, such as her salary, house, and other goods. If this happens, the property must be given back to the woman and the person who took it may be punished with short term imprisonment.

Forced labour (article 36)

Forcing girls and women to engage in forced labor—inside or outside the house—is against the law. "Forced labor" is explained in the Labor Law (article 6) as intimidating, threatening, or otherwise pressuring a person to work against her will. Doing so can subject the person to 6 months in prison.

Marriage of more than one woman (article 37)

It is a crime for a man to marry more than one woman, unless he can make sure to fulfill the three conditions under the Civil Code. Article 86 of the Civil Code requires that 1) the marriage will not cause injustice between the wives, 2) the man can provide for each of the women with food, clothes, a suitable house, and medical treatment, and 3) the first wife must suffer from an incurable disease or be unable to bear children. The punishment for failing to fulfill all three conditions is imprisonment of no less than 3 months.

Denial of relationship (article 38)

If a person tries to deny that a woman is a family member or relative to prevent her from accessing property, inheritance, or other rights, the woman may have her relationship confirmed (validated) by a decision of the court. Denying a relationship with a woman includes, for example, a husband denying a woman is his wife, or an uncle denying his brother's daughter is related to him, a brother denying a woman is his sister, or in-laws denying a woman was married to their son so the woman will not receive inheritance or other legal rights, such as custody or maintenance.

To avoid situations where relatives can deny a woman's relationship to them, it is important for women to have documents that prove their marriages and family relationship. A person who wrongly denies a woman of a family relationship may be punished with up to 6 months in prison.

Denial to Education, Work and Healthcare

Preventing women's access to education, work, and healthcare (article 35)

Preventing or forbidding a girl or a woman from attending school or university, from working outside the home, or from visiting doctors for treatment is a crime. It is against the law for a father, brother, husband, any relative or stranger to prohibit women's access to education, work, or medical care. A person who does that will be punished with up to 6 months in prison.

Appendix B

Agreement on Provisional Arrangements in Afghanistan Pending the Re-Establishment of Permanent Government Institutions

The participants in the UN Talks on Afghanistan,

In the presence of the Special Representative of the Secretary-General for Afghanistan,

Determined to end the tragic conflict in Afghanistan and promote national reconciliation, lasting peace, stability and respect for human rights in the country,

Reaffirming the independence, national sovereignty and territorial integrity of Afghanistan,

Acknowledging the right of the people of Afghanistan to freely determine their own political future in accordance with the principles of Islam, democracy, pluralism and social justice,

Expressing their appreciation to the Afghan mujahidin who, over the years, have defended the independence, territorial integrity and national unity of the country and have played a major role in the struggle against terrorism and oppression, and whose sacrifice has now made them both heroes of jihad and champions of peace, stability and reconstruction of their beloved homeland, Afghanistan,

Aware that the unstable situation in Afghanistan requires the implementation of emergency interim arrangements and expressing their deep appreciation to His Excellency Professor Burhanuddin Rabbani for his readiness to transfer power to an interim authority which is to be established pursuant to this agreement,

Recognizing the need to ensure broad representation in these interim arrangements of all segments of the Afghan population, including groups that have not been adequately represented at the UN Talks on Afghanistan,

Noting that these interim arrangements are intended as a first step toward the establishment of a broad-based, gender-sensitive, multi-ethnic and fully representative government, and are not intended to remain in place beyond the specified period of time,

Recognizing that some time may be required for a new Afghan security force to be fully constituted and functional and that therefore other security provisions detailed in Annex I to this agreement must meanwhile be put in place,

Considering that the United Nations, as the internationally recognised impartial institution, has a particularly important role to play, detailed in Annex II to this agreement, in the period prior to the establishment of permanent institutions in Afghanistan,

Have agreed as follows:

THE INTERIM AUTHORITY

I. General provisions

(1) An Interim Authority shall be established upon the official transfer of power on 22 December 2001.

(2) The Interim Authority shall consist of an Interim Administration presided over by a Chairman, a Special Independent Commission for the Convening of the Emergency Loya Jirga, and a Supreme Court of Afghanistan, as well as such other courts as may be established by the Interim Administration.

The composition, functions and governing procedures for the Interim Administration and the Special Independent Commission are set forth in this agreement.

(3) Upon the official transfer of power, the Interim Authority shall be the repository of Afghan sovereignty, with immediate effect. As such, it shall, throughout the interim period, represent Afghanistan in its external relations and shall occupy the seat of Afghanistan at the United Nations and in its specialised agencies, as well as in other international institutions and conferences.

(4) An Emergency Loya Jirga shall be convened within six months of the establishment of the Interim Authority. The Emergency Loya Jirga will be opened by His Majesty Mohammed Zaher, the former King of Afghanistan. The Emergency Loya Jirga shall decide on a Transitional Authority, including a broad-based transitional administration, to lead Afghanistan until such time as a fully representative government can be elected through free and fair elections to be held no later than two years from the date of the convening of the Emergency Loya Jirga.

(5) The Interim Authority shall cease to exist once the Transitional Authority has been established by the Emergency Loya Jirga.

(6) A Constitutional Loya Jirga shall be convened within eighteen months of the establishment of the Transitional Authority, in order to adopt a new constitution for Afghanistan. In order to assist the Constitutional Loya Jirga prepare the proposed Constitution, the Transitional Administration shall, within two months of its commencement and with the assistance of the United Nations, establish a Constitutional Commission.

II. Legal framework and judicial system

(1) The following legal framework shall be applicable on an interim basis until the adoption of the new Constitution referred to above: i) The Constitution of 1964, a/ to the extent that its provisions are not inconsistent with those contained in this agreement, and b/ with the exception of those provisions relating to the monarchy and to the executive and legislative bodies provided in the Constitution; and ii) existing laws and regulations, to the extent that they are not inconsistent with this agreement or with international legal obligations to

which Afghanistan is a party, or with those applicable provisions contained in the Constitution of 1964, provided that the Interim Authority shall have the power to repeal or amend those laws and regulations.

(2) The judicial power of Afghanistan shall be independent and shall be vested in a Supreme Court of Afghanistan, and such other courts as may be established by the Interim Administration. The Interim Administration shall establish, with the assistance of the United Nations, a Judicial Commission to rebuild the domestic justice system in accordance with Islamic principles, international standards, the rule of law and Afghan legal traditions.

III. Interim Administration

A. Composition

(1) The Interim Administration shall be composed of a Chairman, five Vice Chairmen and 24 other members. Each member, except the Chairman, may head a department of the Interim Administration.

(2) The participants in the UN Talks on Afghanistan have invited His Majesty Mohammed Zaher, the former King of Afghanistan, to chair the Interim Administration. His Majesty has indicated that he would prefer that a suitable candidate acceptable to the participants be selected as the Chair of the Interim Administration.

(3) The Chairman, the Vice Chairmen and other members of the Interim Administration have been selected by the participants in the UN Talks on Afghanistan, as listed in Annex IV to this agreement. The selection has been made on the basis of professional competence and personal integrity from lists submitted by the participants in the UN Talks, with due regard to the ethnic, geographic and religious composition of Afghanistan and to the importance of the participation of women.

(4) No person serving as a member of the Interim Administration may simultaneously hold membership of the Special

Independent Commission for the Convening of the Emergency Loya Jirga.

B. Procedures

(1) The Chairman of the Interim Administration, or in his/her absence one of the Vice Chairmen, shall call and chair meetings and propose the agenda for these meetings.

(2) The Interim Administration shall endeavour to reach its decisions by consensus. In order for any decision to be taken, at least 22 members must be in attendance. If a vote becomes necessary, decisions shall be taken by a majority of the members present and voting, unless otherwise stipulated in this agreement. The Chairman shall cast the deciding vote in the event that the members are divided equally.

C. Functions

(1) The Interim Administration shall be entrusted with the day-to-day conduct of the affairs of state, and shall have the right to issue decrees for the peace, order and good government of Afghanistan.

(2) The Chairman of the Interim Administration or, in his/her absence, one of the Vice Chairmen, shall represent the Interim Administration as appropriate.

(3) Those members responsible for the administration of individual departments shall also be responsible for implementing the policies of the Interim Administration within their areas of responsibility.

4) Upon the official transfer of power, the Interim Administration shall have full jurisdiction over the printing and delivery of the national currency and special drawing rights from international financial institutions. The Interim Administration shall establish, with the assistance of the United Nations, a Central Bank of Afghanistan that will regulate the money supply of the country through transparent and accountable procedures.

(5) The Interim Administration shall establish, with the assistance of the United Nations, an independent Civil Service

Commission to provide the Interim Authority and the future Transitional Authority with shortlists of candidates for key posts in the administrative departments, as well as those of governors and uluswals, in order to ensure their competence and integrity.

(6) The Interim Administration shall, with the assistance of the United Nations, establish an independent Human Rights Commission, whose responsibilities will include human rights monitoring, investigation of violations of human rights, and development of domestic human rights institutions. The Interim Administration may, with the assistance of the United Nations, also establish any other commissions to review matters not covered in this agreement.

(7) The members of the Interim Administration shall abide by a Code of Conduct elaborated in accordance with international standards.

(8) Failure by a member of the Interim Administration to abide by the provisions of the Code of Conduct shall lead to his/her suspension from that body. The decision to suspend a member shall be taken by a twothirds majority of the membership of the Interim Administration on the proposal of its Chairman or any of its Vice Chairmen.

(9) The functions and powers of members of the Interim Administration will be further elaborated, as appropriate, with the assistance of the United Nations.

IV. The Special Independent Commission for the Convening of the Emergency Loya Jirga

(1) The Special Independent Commission for the Convening of the Emergency Loya Jirga shall be established within one month of the establishment of the Interim Authority. The Special Independent Commission will consist of twenty-one members, a number of whom should have expertise in constitutional or customary law. The members will be selected from lists of candidates submitted by participants in the UN Talks on Afghanistan as well as Afghan professional and civil society groups. The United Nations will assist with the

establishment and functioning of the commission and of a substantial secretariat.

(2) The Special Independent Commission will have the final authority for determining the procedures for and the number of people who will participate in the Emergency Loya Jirga. The Special Independent Commission will draft rules and procedures specifying (i) criteria for allocation of seats to the settled and nomadic population residing in the country; (ii) criteria for allocation of seats to the Afghan refugees living in Iran, Pakistan, and elsewhere, and Afghans from the diaspora; (iii) criteria for inclusion of civil society organisations and prominent individuals, including Islamic scholars, intellectuals, and traders, both within the country and in the diaspora. The Special Independent Commission will ensure that due attention is paid to the representation in the Emergency Loya Jirga of a significant number of women as well as all other segments of the Afghan population.

(3) The Special Independent Commission will publish and disseminate the rules and procedures for the convening of the Emergency Loya Jirga at least ten weeks before the Emergency Loya Jirga convenes, together with the date for its commencement and its suggested location and duration.

4) The Special Independent Commission will adopt and implement procedures for monitoring the process of nomination of individuals to the Emergency Loya Jirga to ensure that the process of indirect election or selection is transparent and fair. To pre-empt conflict over nominations, the Special Independent Commission will specify mechanisms for filing of grievances and rules for arbitration of disputes.

(5) The Emergency Loya Jirga will elect a Head of the State for the Transitional Administration and will approve proposals for the structure and key personnel of the Transitional Administration.

V. Final provisions

(1) Upon the official transfer of power, all mujahidin, Afghan armed forces and armed groups in the country shall come

under the command and control of the Interim Authority, and be reorganised according to the requirements of the new Afghan security and armed forces.

(2) The Interim Authority and the Emergency Loya Jirga shall act in accordance with basic principles and provisions contained in international instruments on human rights and international humanitarian law to which Afghanistan is a party.

(3) The Interim Authority shall cooperate with the international community in the fight against terrorism, drugs and organised crime. It shall commit itself to respect international law and maintain peaceful and friendly relations with neighbouring countries and the rest of the international community.

(4) The Interim Authority and the Special Independent Commission for the Convening of the Emergency Loya Jirga will ensure the participation of women as well as the equitable representation of all ethnic and religious communities in the Interim Administration and the Emergency Loya Jirga.

(5) All actions taken by the Interim Authority shall be consistent with Security Council resolution 1378 (14 November 2001) and other relevant Security Council resolutions relating to Afghanistan.

(6) Rules of procedure for the organs established under the Interim Authority will be elaborated as appropriate with the assistance of the United Nations.

This agreement, of which the annexes constitute an integral part, done in Bonn on this 5th day of December 2001 in the English language, shall be the authentic text, in a single copy which shall remain deposited in the archives of the United Nations. Official texts shall be provided in Dari and Pashto, and such other languages as the Special Representative of the Secretary-General may designate. The Special Representative of the Secretary-General shall send certified copies in English, Dari and Pashto to each of the participants.

The Agreement was signed on December 5, 2001 in Bonn, Germany.